Study Guide

for

Newman and Newman's

Development Through Life
A Psychosocial Approach
Ninth Edition

Barbara M. Newman
University of Rhode Island

Philip R. Newman
University of Rhode Island

Laura Landry-Meyer
Bowling Green State University

Brenda J. Lohman
Iowa State University

THOMSON

WADSWORTH

Australia • Brazil • Canada • Mexico • Singapore • Spain • United Kingdom • United States

Printed in the United States of America

1 2 3 4 5 6 7 09 08 07 06 05

Printer: Thomson West

ISBN 0-495-03072-4

Thomson Higher Education
10 Davis Drive
Belmont, CA 94002-3098
USA

For more information about our products, contact us at:
Thomson Learning Academic Resource Center
1-800-423-0563

For permission to use material from this text or product, submit a request online at
http://www.thomsonrights.com.
Any additional questions about permissions can be submitted by email to **thomsonrights@thomson.com.**

TABLE OF CONTENTS

Preface

PREFACE

To the Student:

There are many ways to approach studying for your course in human development depending upon your learning style, your motivation, your background, and the course objectives. The purpose of this *Study Guide* is to provide a variety of strategies for study and to help you focus on key ideas as you read and review. Research has demonstrated that you will improve your mastery of academic material and test performance if you actively engage the material in addition to reading and listening to lectures. Participate in class discussion, meet with other students to talk about your ideas, try to translate concepts into your own words and relate them to your observations or experiences, look for the links among topics and trace patterns or themes across life stages. The more you use the ideas and link them with other information, the more they become a meaningful part of your knowledge base.

The *Study Guide* is not intended to be a substitute for reading the text and other assigned readings suggested by your instructor. The text is not presented in brief here. Rather, we have developed this guide in order to focus your attention on the organization, basic concepts, and underlying issues of each chapter. In addition, we have provided a set of pre-test and post-test questions for each chapter to help strengthen your test-taking skills and to help assess improvement in your mastery of the concepts.

Each chapter of the *Study Guide* follows the same eight-step organization. If you follow these steps, you will have a solid grasp of important information in the text and will find that the concepts become more fully integrated into the way you think and talk about development.

Step One. Before reading the chapter, review the chapter outline. The outline gives a clear idea of the main topics to be covered in the chapter and how they are related to one another.

Step Two. Review the chapter objectives. These objective statements summarize the main goals of each chapter and alert you to important themes.

Step Three. Before reading the chapter, take the 25-item pre-test. This exercise will focus your attention on important ideas. It will also help you appreciate how much additional information you can gain by reading the text. The Answer Key for the pre-test is at the back of the *Study Guide*. Give yourself a score on the pre-test before going on to read the chapter. Use the page numbers cited with each question to find information related to specific questions. The topics covered in the pre-test (and the post-test) are not exhaustive. You should expect to be examined over a much wider range of information than is presented in these tests. However, these tests will give you a starting point for guiding your reading and assessing your growth in knowledge.

Step Four. Read the chapter. As you read, use the chapter objectives and the topics covered in the pre-test to make sure that you are paying attention to main ideas.

Step Five. Review basic concepts by matching each term with its definition. It is good practice to work both from words to their definitions and from definitions to words. This exercise will strengthen your ability to use new vocabulary and differentiate similar concepts. The list does not include all terms introduced in each chapter. It focuses on words that may be unfamiliar or may be used in a specific sense in the chapter. The correct answers for the matching questions are provided in the Answer Key at the end of the *Study Guide*. As you read the chapter, be sure to consider the bold face words. These terms are in the glossary.

Step Six. Answer the focusing questions. These questions are intended to help summarize basic ideas from the text and develop new ideas based on the chapter reading. Use your own words to answer these questions. The more easily you can explain ideas in your own terms, the more confident you can be that you understand them.

Step Seven. Take the 20-item post-test. The post-test questions have more specific information than required in the pre-test. The Answer Key is provided at the end of the *Study Guide*. Be sure to reread the material related to any questions you missed or questions felt uncertain. The difference between pre-test and post-test scores will give you some idea of the effectiveness of your study strategies.

For additional test items, you may want to go to the *Development Through Life* web site found by going to http://wadsworth.com/newman_newman9e. If you still have questions, discuss them with your instructor.

Another helpful tactic is to make up multiple choice questions about topics covered in the text. This strategy forces you to break down information into very specific elements and reframe those elements into questions.

Step Eight. Suggestions for further observation and study are offered as a last step. We hope you will enrich your learning in the course by linking main ideas to your personal observations, experiences, and additional reading. In each chapter, questions are raised about the application of human development research and theory to specific life experiences and challenges. The suggestions offered in the last section of each *Study Guide* chapter draw your attention to these issues in an attempt to build a richer context for your current learning and future study.

Barbara M. Newman
University of Rhode Island

Philip R. Newman
University of Rhode Island

Laura Landry-Meyer
Bowling Green State University

Brenda Lohman
Iowa State University

CHAPTER ONE
The Development Through Life Perspective

Step One: Review Chapter Outline

Step Two: Review the Chapter Objectives

- To introduce the basic assumptions that guide the organization of the text.
- To introduce the psychosocial approach to the study of development, including the interrelationship among the biological, psychological, and societal systems.
- To note historical changes in life expectancy and examine the implications of these changes for the study of development over the life span.

Step Three: Take the Pre-Test

Answer these true/false questions before you read the chapter. The pages where material is discussed are indicated in the parentheses after each question. Use your performance as a guide to areas where you need to read carefully. The Answer Key for the pre-test can be found at the end of the study guide.

_____1.   One assumption of the life span perspective is that growth occurs at every period of life. (p. 5)

_____2.   The life span approach is influenced by physical abilities. (p. 5)

_____3.   The psychosocial approach emphasizes the importance of two systems: the biological system and the psychological system. (p. 6)

_____4.   Individuals' lives show continuity and change throughout time. (p. 5)

_____5.   Changes in the psychological system can be self-directed. (p. 6)

_____6.   Social roles, cultural myths, and political ideologies are processes of the biological system. (p. 7)

_____7.   Poverty is considered a risk factor because it reduces access to basic resources associated with survival. (p. 8)

_____8.   The psychosocial perspective emphasizes the relative importance of the person and the unimportance of the social environment. (pp. 9-10)

_____9.   Internal experiences are products of interaction of biological, psychological, and societal systems. (p. 9)

_____10.   Human development occurs from birth through adolescence. (p. 11)

_____11.   It is best to analyze individual behavior only using the biological system and age. (p. 6)

_____12.   The biological, psychological, and societal systems are responsive and adapt to changes. (pp. 6-7)

_____13.   The biological system can modify the social and psychological systems. (p. 6)

_____14.   Cultural values and rituals have minimal impact on human development. (pp. 7-8)

_____15.   Few societies have age-graded expectations regarding individual development and social roles. (p. 8)

_____16.   Poverty decreases the risks individuals face in their development. (p. 8)

_____17.   The meaning of an event remains the same for individuals over their life course. (pp. 9-10)

_____18.   The primary purpose of making meaning of events is to increase longevity. (p. 10)

_____19.   Lifestyle choices have an impact on development and longevity. (p. 11)

_____20.   People from different cultures have distinct ideas about how one ought to behave at different ages. (p. 11)

_____21.   Historical events, such as the tragedy on September 11, 2001 in New York City with the World Trade Center, have a lasting impact on individuals who were alive at that time period. (pp. 11-12)

_____22.   According to projections, life expectancy has been increasing for all men and women. (p. 12)

_____23.   Life hazards during the early and middle years of life, shorten the average life expectancy at birth. (p. 12)

_____24.   Lifestyle factors are relatively unimportant in increasing one's longevity. (pp. 13-14)

_____25.   Persistent poverty during infancy and childhood are often predictors of resiliency in adulthood. (pp. 8-9)

Step Four: Read Chapter 1: The Development Through Life Perspective

Step Five: Review Basic Concepts By Matching Each Term and Its Definition

a. biological system   b. psychological system
c. societal system   d. psychosocial approach
e. life expectancy   f. resilience

1. _____   The number of years of life, based on average length of life for a given population.

2. _____   A characteristic that buffers the negative effects of poverty.

3. _____   All the processes necessary for thinking and reasoning.

4. _____   A human development theory that emphasizes the interaction of biological, psychological, and societal systems over the life span.

5. _____   All the processes necessary for the physiological functioning of an organism.

6. _____   All the processes through which a person becomes integrated into society.

Step Six: Answer the Focusing Questions

1. List and explain the five major assumptions guiding the focus of the textbook. (p. 5)

2. Identify and describe the three systems. (pp. 6-7)

3.   Explain the relationship between the psychosocial approach and the interaction of the biological, psychological, and societal systems. (pp. 6-7)

4.   Identify and describe the biological, psychological, and societal aspects of poverty. (pp. 8-9)

5.   Define and describe life expectancy and its importance in the study of lifespan human development. (pp. 11-12)

6.   What changes have occurred in life expectancy over this century? (pp. 12-13)

Step Seven: Take the Post-Test

1.   Which of the following statements best reflects the assumptions of the text? (p. 5)
        a.   Personality is fixed by age 6.
        b.   New psychosocial development occurs at every life stage.
        c.   Psychosocial development is complete once identity formation occurs.
        d.   Development in adulthood occurs in the societal system only.

2.   When are growth and change likely to occur? (p. 5)
        a.   during infancy
        b.   during adolescence
        c.   during early adulthood
        d.   during every period of life

3.	The life span approach recognizes _____. (p. 5)
	a.	only individual differences in human development
	b.	only family differences in human development
	c.	patterns of continuity and change from one developmental period to another
	d.	the death rate of people born in the 1900's

4.	An assumption of the text is that we need to seek understanding of the whole person because _____. (p. 7)
	a.	individuals interrelate in a variety of settings and within a variety of relationships
	b.	theories examine individuals, not families
	c.	individuals are isolated in contextual settings
	d.	individuals function in a manner that integrates physical, social, emotional, and cognitive capacities

5.	What are the three major systems that interact to produce human experience? (pp. 6-7)
	a.	biological, psychological, and societal systems
	b.	democratic, capitalist, and socialist systems
	c.	fantasy, reasoning, and the unconscious
	d.	respiratory, circulatory, and metabolic systems

6.	Which system includes all the mental processes central to the person's ability to make meaning of experiences and take action? (p. 6)
	a.	the biological system
	b.	the psychological system
	c.	the societal system
	d.	the scientific system

7.	Which of the following is most likely to bring about change in the biological system? (p. 6)
	a.	use of drugs
	b.	entry into new roles
	c.	movement from one culture to the next
	d.	age graded expectations

8.	Which of the following is most likely to bring about change in the psychological system? (pp. 6-7)
	a.	disease
	b.	environmental toxins
	c.	education
	d.	accidents

9.	Which of the following is most likely to bring about change in the societal system? (pp. 7-8)
	a.	genetic factors
	b.	insight
	c.	nutrition
	d.	entry into new roles

10. The Green Family attended their grandmother's 100th birthday party. Prior to her birthday, grandma lived alone and enjoyed being independent. On her 100th birthday, grandma felt that her memory was gone and ability to live alone was over. Grandma's perception is a product of which of the following systems? (pp. 6-8)
    a. caregiving systems
    b. societal system
    c. biological system
    d. psychological system

11. The Brown Family attended their grandfather's 80th birthday party in which he danced and played games with his grandchildren boasting to live to be 200. Immediately following his party, grandpa fell and broke his hip. His new disability altered his outlook on life and he no longer wanted to interact with family. This example illustrates which of the following? (pp. 6-8)
    a. Older adults should not be active.
    b. The biological system can modify one's psychological outlook on life.
    c. The Brown Family should have taken more care with grandpa's longevity.
    d. The biological system is viewed independently of other systems to predict life expectancy.

12. The tragedy of the World Trade Center in New York City on September 11, 2001 is considered a historical event and can be categorized into what system? (pp. 7-8)
    a. biological
    b. psychological
    c. societal
    d. democratic

13. Which of the following statements about the psychosocial approach is most accurate? (p. 9)
    a. The meaning of life experiences changes over the course of life for individuals.
    b. The meaning of life is only based on an individual's psychological outlook.
    c. Life experiences are dictated by physical maturity.
    d. Personal relationships have little influence on individual development.

14. The psychosocial approach primarily focuses on _____. (p. 10)
    a. longevity of individuals
    b. the impact of poverty on development
    c. cultural values in isolation
    d. the emergence of identity over the life course

15. The impact of poverty is complex and can _____ the risks individuals face in their development. (pp. 8-9)
    a. decrease
    b. increase
    c. stabilize
    d. desensitize

16. The concept of identity best illustrates the relationship between the psychological system and the _____ system. (p. 10)
    a. biological
    b. scientific
    c. adaptive
    d. societal

17. The psychosocial approach focuses on the continuous interaction between individuals and _____. (p. 9)
    a. social environments
    b. families
    c. death
    d. re-birth

18. How is the study of life span human development related to life expectancy? (pp. 11-12).
    a. The study of life span human development only focuses on estimating death rates.
    b. The study of life span human development only focuses on estimating birth rates.
    c. The study of life span human development is independent of life expectancy and has no relationship.
    d. The study of life span human development is dependent upon life expectancy, a framework for timing about stages or periods of life.

19. Which of the following statements most accurately describes projections of life expectancy? (p. 12)
    a. Men can expect to outlive women worldwide.
    b. Life expectancy is projected to decrease for women and increase for men.
    c. Women can expect to outlive men worldwide.
    d. Women outlive men only in Africa.

20. Marilo wants to estimate her life expectancy. What factors should Marilo consider to most accurately project her life expectancy age? (p. 13)
    a. lifestyle, family ancestry
    b. IQ, demographics
    c. religion, lifestyle
    d. income, religion

After completing the post-test, compare your score with your performance on the pre-test. Can you identify areas where significant new learning has taken place? If you still have questions about some sections of the chapter, read them again. Check the glossary. For additional test items, you may want to go to the Development Through Life web site found by going to http://www.psychology.wadsworth.com. If you still have questions, discuss them with your instructor.

Step Eight: Suggestions for Further Observation and Study

1. Consider an older family member's life story. How do the biological, psychological, and societal systems interact in this person's life story and development? How do the three systems interact in your current development?

2.	Project your life expectancy using information in the chapter. Does your projected life expectancy impact your future? How? What life style changes would you be willing to make to increase your chances of living longer?

3.	Search the Internet for life stories or autobiographies of individuals. Focus on how the three systems interact to impact the individual's development.

4.	Read the book, *Having Our Say: The Delaney Sisters' First 100 Years,* written by Sarah and A. Elizabeth Delaney, with Amy Hill Hearth in 1993. This life history of two sisters who are over 100 years old provides an example of how the biological, psychological, and societal systems interact. You can also explore the web site: http://www.havingoursay.com.

5.	Use InfoTrac® College Edition, an online library to explore chapter concepts in more detail. Go to http://www.infotrac-college.com and use the pass code stated on the card with the textbook.

CHAPTER TWO
The Research Process

Step One: Review Chapter Outline

The Scientific Process
      The Positivist Approach to Research
Scientific Observation
      The Qualitative Inquiry Approach to Research
Research Design
      Sampling
            Random Samples
            Stratified Samples
            Matched Groups
            Volunteer Samples
            The Qualitative Approach to Sampling
            Strengths and Weaknesses of Approaches to Sampling
      Research Methods
            Observation
            Case Study
            Interviews
            Surveys and Tests
            Experimentation
Designs for Studying Development
      Retrospective Studies
      Cross-sectional Studies
      Longitudinal Studies
      Cohort Sequential Studies
Evaluating Existing Research
Ethics
Chapter Summary

Step Two: Review the Chapter Objectives

- To define the scientific process, including the positivist and qualitative approaches to inquiry.
- To review issues in research design including sampling, research methods, and designs for studying development.
- To consider the ethical guidelines for conducting research with human subjects.

Step Three: Take the Pre-Test

Answer these true/false questions before you read the chapter. The pages where material is discussed are indicated in the parentheses after each question. Use your performance as a guide to areas where you need to read especially carefully. The Answer Key for the pre-test can be found at the end of the study guide.

_____1.   Patterns which characterize the experience of one cohort of people apply to other groups of people across historical time periods. (p. 18)

_____2.   A good theory contains specific predictions about cause and effect. (p. 19)

_____3.   A researcher can be totally objective about the research topic. (p. 19)

_____4.   Good researchers try hard to discourage other researchers from conducting studies on their research topic. (p. 19)

_____5.   The scientific process creates a body of knowledge that is objective, systematic, and repeatable. (pp. 19-20)

_____6.   In evaluating the results of an experiment, if the results could have been produced by chance factors, the theory would likely be accepted. (p. 20)

_____7.   The qualitative inquiry approach assumes that there are many versions of the truth depending on the information and context. (p. 20)

_____8.   Qualitative inquiry focuses on statistics in order to generalize behavior. (p. 20)

_____9.   Generalizations from the positivistic approach may be refined through observations made by qualitative inquiry. (p. 20)

_____10.   The sample and the nature of the population from which the sample is taken determine the generalizations that may be made from the research findings. (pp. 20-21)

_____11.   In a random sample, each person in the target population has an equal chance of being included in the sample. (p. 21)

_____12.   A volunteer sample involves two or more matched groups that are similar on specific selected characteristics. (p. 21)

_____13.   The findings of clinical studies can usually be generalized to the population as a whole. (p. 23)

_____14.   A strong correlation between high levels of rejection by peers and low grades in school was found in a study. Therefore, one can conclude that being rejected by peers causes poor academic performance. (p. 25)

_____15.   Case studies have been consistently useful in stimulating theory and research in human development. (pp. 25-26)

_____16.   Once an interviewer establishes rapport with the person being interviewed, there is little danger of influencing the subject's responses. (p. 27)

_____17.   One advantage of surveys as a research method is that they allow the comparison of responses by large groups of respondents. (pp. 28-29)

_____18.   Tests are said to be reliable when they provide roughly the same score or assessment each time the person takes the test, provided no intervention has occurred to bring about change. (pp. 29-30)

_____19.   In an experiment, the group that experiences the experimental manipulation or treatment is referred to as the control group. (p. 30)

_____20.   One advantage of experimentation as a research method is that it allows one to make conclusions about causal relationships. (pp. 30-31)

_____21.   The passage of time does not change the significance of certain past events in a person's memory in the retrospective study method. (p. 32)

_____22.   Longitudinal designs have the advantage of allowing researchers to study the course of development of a group of individuals. (p. 33)

_____23.   A cohort sequential design combines the cross-sectional and the longitudinal designs into one method of study. (p. 33)

_____24.   In a study of human development, a researcher is likely to carry out an evaluation of existing research as one method of studying a subject of interest. (pp. 33-34)

_____25.   After conducting a research study, researchers should seek approval from a human subjects review board. (pp. 34-35)

Step Four: Read Chapter 2: The Research Process

Step Five: Review Basic Concepts By Matching Each Term and Its Definition

a.   scientific process   b.   positivist approach
c.   qualitative approach   d.   research design
e.   sampling   f.   research methods
g.   operational definition   h.   ethics
i.   objective   j.   statistically significant
k.   generalizability   l.   correlation

1.   _____   Principles of morality that guide conduct.

2.   _____   An observation that has a low probability of occurring by chance.

3.   _____   Components of a research project that includes sample, methods, how often data will be collected, and use of data analysis techniques.

4.   _____   A method for systematically building a body of information and evaluating the accuracy of information.

5.   _____   Assumption that research findings are applicable to a population.

6.   _____   Applies statistical analysis to predict outcomes and determine causal relationships.

7.   _____   Relationship among variables based on strength and direction.

8. _____ Translation of an abstract concept into a procedure that is observable and measurable.

9. _____ Emphasizes individual perspectives and a process to understand a unique event.

10. _____ Process of choosing participants for a research study.

11. _____ An observation accurately reflects events.

12. _____ Various techniques and strategies used to gather data.

Step Six: Answer the Focusing Questions

1. What is the relationship between the positivistic and qualitative approach as in the scientific process? (pp. 18-20)

2. Explain the qualitative inquiry method and its processes. (p. 20)

3. Explain the three qualities of scientific observation. (pp. 19-20)

4. Explain the principles of research design. (pp. 20-23)

5. What are the implications for generalizability of each of the five approaches to sampling? (pp. 20-23)

6. What are the strengths and weaknesses of each of the five general research categories? (pp. 23-31)

7. Describe how each of the four designs for studying human development account for patterns of change and continuity. (pp. 31-33)

8. What are the most important ethical principles in conducting research on human subjects? (pp. 34-35)

Step Seven: Take the Post-Test

1. Which parts of the scientific process allow us to determine whether a theory is correct? (p. 19)
    a. constructing the theory
    b. operationalizing the theory
    c. testing the theory and evaluating the results
    d. accepting the theory

2.   Scientific observation differs from personal observation in that it aims to be_____. (pp. 19-20)
        a.   repeatable, immediate, and subjective
        b.   objective, random, and isolated
        c.   subjective, repeatable, and systematic
        d.   objective, repeatable, and systematic

3.   Categories and definitions that are assumed to be meaningful from a positivistic perspective are more _____ when viewed through a qualitative perspective. (p. 20)
        a.   ambiguous
        b.   concrete
        c.   systematic
        d.   operational

4.   Dr. Samm utilizes a positivistic approach to research. In other words, she _____. (p. 20)
        a.   makes observations and records them
        b.   uses hypotheses to guide the research process
        c.   has an optimistic outlook about her sample
        d.   gathers data with positively worded survey questions

5.   In a research study, every sample is _____. (p. 21)
        a.   generalizable to all people
        b.   culturally relevant
        c.   taken from a population
        d.   heterogeneous in all characteristics

6.   A researcher wants to compare grandparents who email their grandchildren and grandparents who do not email their grandchildren. Which of the following sampling methods would be ideal to compare the grandparents? (p. 22)
        a.   A random sample of grandparents in the United States.
        b.   A volunteer sample of grandparents in the town where the researcher works.
        c.   A random sample of grandparents in the United States who have access to the Internet.
        d.   A matched sample of grandparents who do and do not have access to the Internet.

7.   Which research methods are best suited for qualitative inquiry? (p. 22)
        a.   surveys, tests
        b.   structured interviews, surveys
        c.   observation, case studies
        d.   tests, observation

8.   Researchers made videotapes and took notes while fathers fed, bathed, and comforted their infants in their homes. Which of the following best describes the research method being used? (p. 23)
        a.   experimentation
        b.   naturalistic observation
        c.   survey
        d.   case study

9.	Which of the following is NOT considered a sampling procedure? (pp. 21-23)
	a.	random
	b.	matched
	c.	quasi experimental
	d.	stratified

10.	Although a scholar may believe that his or her research findings are relevant to a wide group of people, the generalizability of the findings is usually limited to _____. (pp. 21-22)
	a.	the sample and the population from which the sample is drawn
	b.	the people living in the researcher's city
	c.	the people who participated in the study
	d.	people of the same race and sex as the sample

11.	Dr. Phil wants to ensure that his sample is representative of the population. Which sampling methods should he use? (pp. 21-22)
	a.	volunteer and matched
	b.	random and matched
	c.	qualitative and stratified
	d.	stratified and random

12.	Based on data, a correlation of .70 was found between creativity and the number of hours per week children are in full-time child care. What does this correlation mean? (p. 25)
	a.	There is a strong positive relationship between creativity and time spent in child care.
	b.	Creativity is a result of good child care programs.
	c.	There is a negative relationship between creativity and children in child care.
	d.	Child care is a barrier to creativity in children.

13.	Which research method has as one of its weaknesses achieving interobserver reliability? (pp. 25-26)
	a.	case study
	b.	observation
	c.	interview
	d.	surveys

14.	If you carried out an in-depth analysis of a single person or a family, gathering data from many sources, you would be using which of the following research methods? (p. 26)
	a.	experimentation
	b.	survey research
	c.	naturalistic observation
	d.	case study

15.	Which of the following is NOT an advantage of the experimental method? (pp. 29-31)
	a.	It captures what happens naturally in the person's life settings.
	b.	It permits the researcher to isolate and control specific variables.
	c.	It allows one to compare the impact of specific treatments.
	d.	It leads to statements about causal relationships.

16.   What is a cross-sectional research study? (p. 32)
        a.   a naturalistic observation
        b.   a study that follows the same people over time
        c.   a study that compares different groups of people at one time
        d.   a study that uses only surveys as a source of data, not observation or interviews

17.   Why is the cohort sequential design an improvement over the cross-sectional design? (pp. 31-33)
        a.   It allows one to study people who were the same age at three different times.
        b.   It follows the same individuals over repeated observations across time.
        c.   It takes a lot longer to complete the cohort sequential research design.
        d.   It encourages participants to think back about earlier periods in their life.

18.   Which of the following designs involves repeated observations of the same group of people at different times? (p. 33)
        a.   sequential
        b.   longitudinal
        c.   cross-sectional
        d.   retrospective

19.   Dr. Good is on a panel reviewing research proposals. He looks at each proposal and asks, "Is the stress or pain inflicted on participants worth the benefit to society from the potential results?" This is an example of which of the following scientific concerns? (pp. 34-35)
        a.   operational definition
        b.   theoretical framework
        c.   ethics
        d.   objectivity

20.   In designing a research study, which of the following would you use to decide if the procedures were considered ethical? (p. 34)
        a.   how you would feel if you or one of your family members were a participant in this study
        b.   an attorney
        c.   the value and importance of the results
        d.   ask participants after the study has been completed

After completing the post-test, compare your score with your performance on the pre-test. Can you identify areas where significant new learning has taken place? If you still have questions about some sections of the chapter, read them again. Check the glossary. For additional test items, you may want to go to the *Development Through Life* web site found by going to http://www.psychology.wadsworth.com. If you still have questions, discuss them with your instructor.

Step Eight: Suggestions for Further Observation and Study

1.   Select a human development topic of interest to you. Use InfoTrac® to find a peer reviewed, research article focusing on this topic. Evaluate the research based on information in this chapter.

2.   Start with a puzzling observation, something of interest to you. Think of how you might study this question using each of the research methods: observation, case study, interview, surveys, tests, and experimentation. Which approach seems best-suited to the topic you have in mind?

3.   Search the National Institutes of Health, Office of Human Subjects Research (http://ohsr.od.nih.gov/) to learn more about policies that protect human subjects.

4.   Use the American Psychological Association website (http://www.apa.org/) to link to various journals. Review instructions to authors and for reviewers to learn more about the peer review process.

5.   Learning through Technology: InfoTrac®
        For further study, explore InfoTrac® College Edition, an online library. Go to http://www.infotrac-college.com and use the pass code that came on the card with your book. To learn more, look up the following search terms and subdivisions in InfoTrac®.

SCIENTIFIC PROCESS

RESEARCH DESIGN

RESEARCH METHODS
        Interviews
        Case Study
        Research Surveys and Tests
        Experimental Design

RESEARCH ETHICS

PSYCHOLOGICAL RESEARCH
        Methodology
        Psychological Tests

CHAPTER THREE
Psychosocial Theory

Step One: Review the Chapter Outline

Step Two: Review the Chapter Objectives

- To define the concept of theory and explain how one makes use of theory to increase understanding.
- To define the six basic concepts of psychosocial theory.
- To demonstrate how the concepts of psychosocial theory contribute to an analysis of basic processes that foster or inhibit development over the lifespan.
- To evaluate psychosocial theory, pointing out its strengths and weaknesses.

Step Three: Take the Pre-Test

Answer these true/false questions before you read the chapter. The pages where material is discussed are indicated in the parentheses after each question. Use your performance as a guide to areas where you need to read especially carefully. The Answer Key for the pre-test can be found at the end of the study guide.

_____ 1.   The assumptions of a theory are usually stated as testable propositions. (p. 38)

_____ 2.   Psychosocial theory considers individual development within the larger perspective of psychosocial evolution. (pp. 39-40)

_____ 3.   Psychosocial theory assumes that individuals can contribute to their development. (p. 39)

_____ 4.   Psychosocial theory assumes that the most critical period for psychological development is infancy. (p. 39)

_____ 5.   Psychosocial theory views the role of culture as critical in shaping the process and direction of development. (p. 39)

_____ 6.   Stage theories generally propose that there is a specific direction to development. (p. 40)

_____ 7.   An assumption of psychosocial theory and other stage theories is that an individual begins fresh with each new stage. Events of one stage have no bearing on growth at the next stage. (p. 40)

_____ 8.   The concept of psychosocial stages can be traced to psychosexual stages proposed by Freud. (p. 40)

_____ 9.   The textbook, _Development Through Life_, focuses on 11 stages of development. The increase in the number of stages is an extension of Erik Erikson's original 8-stage theory. (p. 41)

_____ 10. There are age restrictions placed on each stage of psychosocial development. (pp. 42-43)

_____ 11. According to psychosocial theory, each developmental stage lasts for the same amount of time in each person's life. (p. 43)

_____ 12. Individuals can review and reinterpret earlier stages bringing new meaning and a change to the resolution of crisis of previous stages. (pp. 42-43)

_____ 13. The concept of developmental tasks suggests that society has age-graded expectations for new levels of mastery at various life stages of development. (p. 43)

_____ 14. Once the sensitive period for acquiring an ability has passed, no new learning of that ability can take place. (p. 43)

_____ 15. At every stage, a person is working on several developmental tasks at once. (pp. 43-44)

_____ 16. Failure to master the competencies of a developmental task in one stage leads to greater difficulty mastering developmental tasks in later stages. (p. 43)

_____ 17. The age-graded demands for growth differ based on a societal or community orientation and value system. (pp. 44-45)

_____ 18. According to psychosocial theory, most people experience only the positive resolution or pole of a psychosocial crisis. (pp. 44-47)

_____ 19. One of the most useful features of psychosocial theory is that the psychosocial crisis is the same at every stage of life. (pp. 44-47)

_____ 20. In psychosocial theory, tension and conflict are necessary to the developmental process. (p. 47)

_____ 21. The progression of psychosocial crises throughout a life course occurs in unpredictable patterns. (pp. 47-48)

_____ 22. The concept, central process refers to the acquisition of new skills and successful coping mechanisms in order to resolve a psychosocial crisis. (pp. 47-48)

_____ 23. According to psychosocial theory, the network of significant relationships remains unchanged throughout the lifespan. (p. 48)

_____ 24. A person's adaptive ego qualities contribute to that person's worldview which is continuously reformulated to accommodate new adaptive ego qualities. (p. 52)

_____ 25. A sense of competence toward the interpretation of life is considered a core pathology. (p. 52)

Step Four: Read Chapter 3: Psychosocial Theory

Step Five: Review Basic Concepts By Matching Each Term and Its Definition

a.	theory	b.	psychosocial theory
c.	developmental stage	d.	developmental tasks
e.	coping	f.	central process
g.	psychosocial crisis	h.	radius of significant relationships
i.	core pathologies	j.	prime adaptive ego qualities

1. _____ A theory of human development which proposes that cognitive, emotional, and social growth are a product of the interaction between social expectations at each life stage and the competencies people bring to each life challenge.

2. _____ A predictable tension between personal competencies and social expectations.

3. _____ Mental states that emerge in the positive resolution of each psychosocial crisis which form a basic orientation toward the interpretation of life experiences.

4. _____ Active efforts to keep stress at a manageable level.

5. _____ Skills and competence that are acquired at each stage of development.

6. _____ Destructive forces that result from severe, negative resolutions of each psychosocial crisis.

7. _____ The predominant mechanism through which a psychosocial crisis is resolved.

8. _____ A period of life that is characterized by some underlying organization or emphasis.

9. _____ The range of important interpersonal bonds through which social expectations reach the person and from which the person derives essential social support.

10. _____ A logical system of concepts that provides a framework for organizing and understanding observations.

Step Six: Answer the Focusing Questions

1. What questions must one ask in order to understand a theory? How would you answer each question from the perspective of psychosocial theory? (p. 38)

2. What four questions should a theory of human development address? How does psychosocial theory address these issues? (p. 39)

3. Explain how each of the basic concepts of psychosocial theory operates to produce development at each stage of life. (pp. 39-53)

4. Explain three strengths and three weaknesses of psychosocial theory. (pp. 54-58)

Step Seven: Take the Post-Test

1. Which term refers to a logical system of general concepts that provides a framework for organizing and understanding observations? (p. 38)
    a. a prediction
    b. an assumption
    c. a matrix
    d. a theory

2. One of the central functions of a _____ is to describe unobservable mechanisms or structures and relate them to one another and to observable events. (p. 38)
    a. psychosocial crisis
    b. developmental task
    c. theory
    d. coping strategy

3. A theory of development helps to explain _____. (p. 38)
    a. how people change and grow over time
    b. causal relationships
    c. how people can predict future behavior
    d. correlational relationships

4. Psychosocial theory focuses on the interaction between individual needs and abilities and _____. (p. 39)
    a. early adulthood
    b. experiences in a variety of other cultures
    c. social expectations and demands
    d. logical reasoning

5. Which of the following statements is considered an assumption of psychosocial theory? (p. 39)
    a. Development is primarily a product of genetic factors.
    b. Individuals have the capacity to contribute to their development.
    c. The basic accomplishments of development are resolved by early adolescence.
    d. Chronological age is the most significant marker of psychological maturity.

6. A _____ is a period of life that is characterized by a specific underlying organization. (p. 40)
    a. developmental stage
    b. developmental task
    c. psychosocial crisis
    d. core pathology

7. According to psychosocial theory, which of the following statements best describes a developmental stage? (pp. 40-41)
    a. Stages follow strict age guidelines.
    b. Stages form a sequence of development based only on genetics.
    c. Stages are the same for all individuals regardless of culture.
    d. Stages can be re-experienced and offer hope if a negative resolution emerges.

8.   Which of the following examples best illustrates the idea of a *sensitive period*? (p. 43)
      a.   Mario is 5 years old and gets his feelings hurt easily if his behavior is criticized.
      b.   Language is more readily learned during the first four years of life; afterward it becomes more difficult to acquire language skills.
      c.   At age 65, Fred is experiencing hearing loss, but doesn't want hearing aids because they are a sign of aging.
      d.   Each life stage has characteristics that differentiate it from the one before and the one after.

9.   Which of the following statements best describes Erikson's view of stages of development? (p. 42)
      a.   Each stage is independent and unrelated to the next.
      b.   Stages form a sequence.
      c.   Stages do not follow a biological plan.
      d.   The themes of one stage are not revisited or reinterpreted in future stages.

10.   In psychosocial theory, a developmental task is considered a _____. (pp. 43-44)
      a.   stage of development
      b.   set of polar tensions
      c.   set of skills and competencies
      d.   social role

11.   Which of the following terms refers to the tension between the person's competencies at the beginning of a stage and social expectations for how one ought to function at that period of life? (p. 44)
      a.   psychosocial theory
      b.   psychosocial stage
      c.   psychosocial environment
      d.   psychosocial crisis

12.   Mastery of developmental tasks is most influenced by _____. (pp. 44-45)
      a.   age of the individual
      b.   resolution of previous psychosocial crises
      c.   the theoretical perspective
      d.   teachable moments

13.   A *psychosocial crisis* is best defined by which of the following? (p. 44)
      a.   Tension state caused by discrepancies between individual competencies and society's expectations.
      b.   The loss of reality testing abilities as a result of a severe trauma.
      c.   Mental state that emerges at each stage creating a positive orientation toward life experiences.
      d.   An interpersonal bond that can be maintained or broken across stages of life.

14.   The _____ for resolving the psychosocial crisis at each life stage provides personal and societal mechanisms for taking in new information and reorganizing existing information. (p. 47)
      a.   developmental stage
      b.   core pathology
      c.   central process
      d.   social support

15. The radius of significant relationships in psychosocial theory _____. (p. 48)
    a. places age-related demands on individuals that are communicated through important social relationships
    b. is a network of distant acquaintances
    c. has little impact on an individual's development
    d. incorporates the genetic influence on development into increasingly complex biological systems

16. At each stage of development, the person has the capacity to engage in a changing network of meaningful social relationships. These social relationships refer to which of the following concepts? (p. 49)
    a. prime adaptive ego qualifications
    b. coping relationships
    c. radius of significant relationships
    d. ethnicity

17. Stefan grew up celebrating Kwanza and Christmas based on cultural influences on his family. His family shared socially standardized ways to celebrate these holidays based on their _____. (p. 50)
    a. stage of development
    b. teachable moments
    c. ethnic group membership
    d. coping mechanisms

18. After five years of marriage, Ken recently divorced his wife. After a period of grief and withdrawal, Ken decided to join a support group. He is also taking college classes to focus on a career and has started a regular exercise program to relieve stress and improve his confidence. Which of the following concepts best describe Ken's behaviors? (p. 50)
    a. coping
    b. psychosocial development stage
    c. central processing
    d. significant relationship construction

19. Which of the following is considered a strength of psychosocial theory? (pp. 54-55)
    a. It highlights the dynamics of family development.
    b. Psychosocial crises allow for the examination of the tension between individual and society.
    c. Infancy and toddlerhood are key periods of development.
    d. The stages of development are patterned after non-Western theories of self and society.

20. What phenomena is psychosocial theory trying to explain? (p. 58)
    a. Changes in problem solving capacity and intelligence.
    b. Changes in sexual motivation and drives.
    c. Changes in habits and other behavior modifications
    d. Changes in self-understanding, social relationships, and worldview.

After completing the post-test, compare your score with your performance on the pre-test. Can you identify areas where significant new learning has taken place? If you still have questions about some sections of the chapter, read them again. Check the glossary. For additional test items, you may want to go to the *Development Through Life* web site found by going to http://www.psychology.wadsworth.com. If you still have questions, discuss them with your instructor.

Step Eight: Suggestions for Further Observation and Study

1.   Read more about Erik Erikson and his works:
   - Coles, R. (1970). *Erik H. Erikson: The growth of his works*. Boston: Atlantic-Little Brown.
   - Erikson, E. H. (1963). *Childhood and society*. (2nd edition). New York: W. W. Norton.
   - Gross, F. L., Jr. (1987). *Introducing Erik Erikson: An invitation to his thinking*. New York: University Press of America.

2.   Search the Internet for information about Erik Erikson. Explore various sites to learn about his life experiences.

3.   Review the stages of development. What are some experiences that are unique to each age group? How does society treat individuals in each age that might suggest that they are members of a common stage of life?

4.   Consider the various rings in the radius of significant relationships. For each ring, list two or three ways that you are influenced by individuals in that sphere. As examples, individuals at each level might have unique expectations for your behavior, serve as sources of encouragement or support, or provide opportunities for new learning.

5.   Identify your own life stage and consider your progress on the developmental tasks of the preceding stage, the current stage, and the following stage. How confident are you about your mastery of the issues in these three adjoining stages? How would you describe your resolution of the crises in these three stages? What kinds of experiences might help you move to a new level of mastery around the issues of your life stage?

6.   Select an area that causes you high levels of stress. How do you try to handle the demands of this situation? Can you think of any new ways that you might handle the situation that might be more successful than what you currently do?

7.   Learning through Technology: InfoTrac®
        For further study, explore InfoTrac® College Edition, an online library. Go to
        http://www.infotrac-college.com and use the pass code that came on the card with your book. To learn more, look up the following search terms and subdivisions in InfoTrac®.

        PSYCHOSOCIAL THEORY

        ERIK ERIKSON

        STAGES OF DEVELOPMENT
                Life Cycle
                Life Stages

        DEVELOPMENTAL TASKS

CHAPTER FOUR
Major Theories for Understanding Human Development

Step One: Review the Chapter Outline

Step Two: Review the Chapter Objectives

- To review the basic concepts of seven major theories that have guided research in the study of human development. These theories include: evolutionary theory; psychosexual theory; cognitive developmental theory, theories of learning, cultural theory; social role theory; and systems theory.
- To examine the implications of each theory for the study of human development.

- To clarify the links between each theory and psychosocial theory.

Step Three: Take the Pre-Test

Answer these true/false questions before you read the chapter. The pages where material is discussed are indicated in the parentheses after each question. Use your performance as a guide to areas where you need to read especially carefully. The Answer Key for the pre-test can be found at the end of the study guide.

_____ 1.   The theory of evolution focuses on species change over long periods of time. (p. 62)

_____ 2.   Psychosocial evolution is a term to describe how human beings create and transmit I Information that influences their adaptation from one generation to the next. (p. 64)

_____ 3.   Freud's psychosexual theory suggests that children have strong sexual drives that influence their mental life. (p. 65)

_____ 4.   The ego tries to gratify superego impulses without generating strong feelings of guilt from the id. (pp. 65-66)

_____ 5.   According to psychosexual theory, many aspects of mental life, including dreams, wishes, and fantasies are not especially meaningful. They are typically products of random brain activity or fatigue. (p. 67)

_____ 6.   According to psychosexual theory, the most important period of life for shaping personality development is early adulthood. (p. 67)

_____ 7.   Both psychosexual theory and psychosocial theory describe stages of development during which qualitative change occurs in a person's social relationships. (pp. 67-68)

_____ 8.   A premise of cognitive developmental theory is that infants, toddlers, young children and adolescents all use the same basic strategies for making meaning of experiences. (p. 68)

_____ 9.   Cognitive developmental theory suggests that knowledge expands and is reorganized through a process of adaptation. (pp. 68-69)

_____ 10.   Vygotsky's theory of cognitive development emphasized the role of social interaction and culture in shaping cognition. (p. 70)

_____ 11.   Vygotsky argued that parents and teachers were relatively unimportant in guiding the development of thought since the emergence of thinking is biologically and genetically controlled. (p. 71-72)

_____ 12.   Classical conditioning and operant conditioning both focus on trial and error learning and the consequences of behavior. (pp. 73-74)

_____ 13.   According to the theory of operant conditioning, the environment can control behavior by setting up systematic contingencies for desired and undesired actions. (pp. 74-75)

_____ 14. According to social learning theory, most of what children learn is a result of direct reinforcement. (pp. 75-76)

_____ 15. Social learning theory offers the view that much learning can occur without direct reinforcement as people observe and imitate the behavior of others. (p. 75-76)

_____ 16. The cognitive behaviorist view of learning argues that mental representations of the learning situation are acquired during the learning process even though they may not be expressed in behavior. (pp. 76-77)

_____ 17. Of all the learning theories discussed in the text, cognitive behaviorism places the greatest emphasis on the way the environment strengthens, shapes, or eliminates behaviors through reinforcement. (pp. 76-77)

_____ 18. According to the theory of cultural determinism, biological similarities among humans far outweigh cultural differences in determining patterns of personal development. (p. 78)

_____ 19. Cultural determinism is a concept developed by Ruth Benedict which refers to the power of culture to shape individual experience. (p. 78)

_____ 20. The influence of ethnic group norms and values on individual development is consistent ` across all members of the group, regardless of their ethnic identification. (p. 79)

_____ 21. The concept of social roles contradicts the view in psychosocial theory that people in various stages of life are interdependent. (pp. 81-82)

_____ 22. Role strain is the sense of overload that results when too many expectations are associated with a role. (pp. 81-82)

_____ 23. According to systems theory, a system can be fully understood by examining the characteristics of each of the component parts. (pp. 82-83)

_____ 24. Open systems maintain their boundaries and their basic identity even though elements and substructures within the system are constantly changing. (pp. 83-84)

_____ 25. The concept of family boundaries refers to all those who are legally associated with a family through blood, marriage, and/or adoption. (pp. 85-86)

Step Four: Read Chapter 4: Major Theories for Understanding Human Development

Step Five: Review Basic Concepts By Matching Each Term and Its Definition

a.	natural selection	b.	ethology
c.	psychosocial evolution	d.	unconscious
e.	ego	f.	equilibrium
g.	classical conditioning	h.	zone of proximal development
i.	operant conditioning	j.	vicarious reinforcement
k.	cognitive map	l.	cultural determinism
m.	open systems	n.	mesosystem

1. _____ Psychological development is shaped by cultural expectations, resources, and challenges.

2. _____ Structures that maintain their organization even though their parts are constantly changing.

3. _____ Comparative study of unique adaptive behaviors that contribute to species' survival.

4. _____ The creation of new information and methods for passing that information from one generation to the next.

5. _____ Learning that occurs when events take place close together in time and thus acquire a similar meaning.

6. _____ A process that accounts for how species change in response to changing environmental conditions over long periods of time.

7. _____ Reality oriented functions such as reasoning, remembering, and planning.

8. _____ A balance in the organization of mental structures that provides the person with effective ways of interpreting experience and interacting with the environment.

9. _____ The interrelationships among two or more settings in which a person participates.

10. _____ The distance between the actual level of development and the level one can achieve when guided by a more capable teacher or peer.

11. _____ Learning that is guided by observing the consequences of the behavior for others.

12. _____ An area of mental functioning and a storehouse of wishes and drives of which one is unaware.

13. _____ An internal mental representation of the learning environment.

14. _____ Learning that emerges as a result of repetition and reinforcement.

Step Six: Answer the Focusing Questions

1. How are the concepts of evolutionary theory, which focus on species adaptation over long periods of time, related to the issues of human development within a single lifetime? (pp. 63-64)

2.   Each of the seven theories places a slightly different emphasis on biological/hereditary factors and environmental factors in accounting for development. For example, cultural theory places emphasis on the role of the environment. For each theory, briefly state the role given to heredity, the role given to environment and the role given to the relationship between heredity and environment. (pp. 63-65)

3.   What do the learning theories, social role theory, and cultural theory have in common? (pp. 73-82)

4.   Of all the theories discussed in Chapter 4, which ones seem to be most closely related to psychosocial theory? What does psychosocial theory add to the study of development that these theories do not provide? (pp. 63-86)

Step Seven: Take the Post-Test

1.   Which of the following terms from evolutionary theory refers to the process by which living organisms adapt to changing environmental conditions over long periods of time? (p. 62)
   a.   assimilation
   b.   natural selection
   c.   cultural determinism
   d.   metacognition

2.   According to evolutionary theory, what is the adaptive consequence of variability for the species? (pp. 62-63)
        a.   promotion of cognitive complexity
        b.   insurance of species survival under varying environmental conditions
        c.   encouragement of responsive parenting
        d.   promotion of helping behavior and cooperation among group members

3.   According to psychosexual theory, what are the three components of personality? (p. 65)
        a.   id, ego, superego
        b.   oral, anal, phallic
        c.   repression, denial, reaction formation
        d.   unconscious, preconscious, conscious

4.   Which of the following theories argues for stages of development? (pp. 65-66)
        a.   classical conditioning
        b.   evolutionary theory
        c.   psychosexual theory
        d.   social role theory

5.   Which of the following is considered a similarity between psychosexual theory and psychosocial theory? (p. 67)
        a.   focus primarily on development up through age 6 as the critical time for change
        b.   emphasize the centrality of sexual impulses as the major area of conflict in development
        c.   view middle childhood as a time for consolidation when little occurs in personality development
        d.   describe changes in the development and capacity of the ego system

6.   A basic assumption of Piaget's cognitive development theory is that an organism strives to achieve _____. (pp. 68-69)
        a.   equilibrium
        b.   autonomy
        c.   conversation
        d.   object permanence

7.   Piaget's cognitive developmental theory focuses on _____. (p. 68)
        a.   id, ego, superego
        b.   how individuals come to 'know' and the emergence of knowledge
        c.   social interactions within a radius of significant others
        d.   solely on the brain development in the first three years

8.   Which of the following is considered a basic concept underlying Vygotsky's theory? (p. 70)
        a.   equilibrium
        b.   unconsciousness
        c.   sexual drives and motivations
        d.   culture

9. Vygostky's contribution to human development is the emphasis on _____. (pp. 70-72)
   a. distance learning
   b. social context
   c. stimulus and response mechanisms
   d. control of sexual impulses

10. Which of the following is considered one of the theories of learning? (p. 73)
   a. evolutionary
   b. cultural
   c. operant conditioning
   d. psychosexual

11. Pavlov's theory of _____ explains events that take place close together in time acquire similar meaning. (p. 73)
   a. social learning
   b. operant conditioning
   c. classical conditioning
   d. cognitive behaviorism

12. What is a *negative reinforcer*? (p. 74)
   a. A stimulus that increases the rate of response when it is present.
   b. A stimulus that increases the rate of response when it is removed.
   c. A stimulus that has the same meaning as the ongoing behavior.
   d. A stimulus that is associated with another stimulus.

13. The focus of social learning theory is that learning _____. (pp. 75-76)
   a. takes place because of schedules of reinforcement
   b. is the result of the interdependence of systems
   c. results from observing and imitating other people's behaviors
   d. is motivated by sexual and aggressive drives

14. Which learning theory focuses on the internal mental activities that influence behavior? (pp. 76-78)
   a. classical conditioning
   b. operant conditioning
   c. social interaction
   d. cognitive behaviorism

15. Which of the following would be considered an example of cultural continuity? (p. 78)
   a. Children take care of younger siblings and then grow up to take care of their children.
   b. All children must learn the proper place and manners associated with elimination.
   c. Children are told not to fight, but at age 16 they are required to enlist in the army.
   d. Some societies restrict access to certain knowledge to a small group of 'healers'.

16. Which term applies to the situation where children are barred from activities that are open to adults or where they have to unlearn behaviors that are appropriate for children but inappropriate for adults? (pp. 78-79)
    a. cultural continuity
    b. cultural relativism
    c. cultural discontinuity
    d. cultural conditioning

17. Which concept from social role theory clarifies why the development and well being of children and adults are so interdependent? (p. 81)
    a. Adults have many more roles than children.
    b. Children are not as identified with their roles as are adults.
    c. Adults and children are often in reciprocal roles.
    d. One experiences more role strain with each stage of life.

18. In social role theory, meaning is derived _____. (pp. 81-82)
    a. through role enactment and integration of behavior
    b. from biologically determined growth and development patterns
    c. through a natural self selection process determine by role strain
    d. from growth patterns in a controlled environment

19. Among the theories presented, which theory places the greatest emphasis on the interdependence of elements and the multidimensional sources of influence on individuals? (p. 82)
    a. evolutionary theory
    b. cognitive developmental theory
    c. psychosexual theory
    d. systems theory

20. Which of the following theories focuses on the processes and relationships among interconnected components of organizations? (p. 82)
    a. psychosexual theory
    b. evolutionary theory
    c. systems theory
    d. cognitive behaviorism

After completing the post-test, compare your score with your performance on the pre-test. Can you identify areas where significant new learning has taken place? If you still have questions about some sections of the chapter, read them again. Check the glossary. For additional test items, you may want to go to the *Development Through Life* web site found by going to http://www.psychology.wadsworth.com. If you still have questions, discuss them with your instructor.

Step Eight: Suggestions for Further Observation and Study

1. Which of the seven theories presented in the chapter comes closest to your personal theory of human behavior? Where did you learn these ideas? Which one is least familiar to you? Examine the ideas in that theory and relate them to what you already know.

2. Read biographical material about two of the theorists discussed in the chapter. What were some historical and intellectual forces that influenced the direction of their thinking? What life events may have channeled their interests toward the study of human behavior?

3. Learning through Technology: InfoTrac®
   For further study, explore InfoTrac® College Edition, an online library. Go to http://www.infotrac-college.com and use the pass code that came on the card with your book. To learn more, look up the following search terms and subdivisions in InfoTrac®.

EVOLUTIONARY THEORY	THEORIES OF LEARNING
	Classical Conditioning
PSYCHOANLYATIC THEORY	Social Learning Theory
PIAGETIAN THEORY OF COGNITIVE DEVELOPMENT	CULTURAL THEORY
	SOCIAL ROLE THEORY
VYGOTSKY	
Zone of Proximal Development	SYSTEMS THEORY

CHAPTER FIVE
The Period of Pregnancy and Prenatal Development

Step One: Review the Chapter Outline

Genetics and Development
    Genes and Chromosomes as Sources of Genetic Information
    The Laws of Heredity
    Genetic Sources of Individual Differences
    Genetic Technology and Psychosocial Evolution
    Evaluating the Contribution of Genetic Factors to Behavior
Normal Fetal Development
    Fertilization
    Development in the First Trimester
    Development in the Second Trimester
    Development in the Third Trimester
The Birth Process
    Stages of Labor
    Cesarean Delivery
    Infant Mortality
The Mother, the Fetus, and the Psychosocial Environment
    The Impact of the Fetus on the Pregnant Woman
Case Study: A Father's Recollections about his Daughter's Birth
    The Impact of the Pregnant Woman on the Fetus
    The Cultural Context of Pregnancy and Childbirth
        Reactions to Pregnancy
        Reactions to Childbirth
Applied Topic: Abortion
    The Legal Context of Abortion in the United States
    The Incidence of Legal Abortions
    The Psychosocial Impact of Abortion on Women
Case Study: Karen and Don
Chapter Summary

Step Two: Review the Chapter Objectives

- To describe the biochemical basis of genetic information and the process through which genetic information is transmitted from one generation to the next.
- To identify the contributions of genetic factors to individuality through their role in controlling the rate of development, their contributions to individual traits, and the genetic sources of abnormalities.
- To trace fetal development through three trimesters of pregnancy, including an understanding of critical periods of sensitivity to agents that may interfere with normal fetal development.
- To describe the birth process and factors that contribute to infant mortality.
- To analyze the reciprocity between the pregnant woman and the developing fetus, focusing on ways that pregnancy affects a childbearing woman and expectant father, as well as basic influences on fetal growth such as maternal age, drug use, nutrition, environmental toxins, and the impact of poverty.

- To examine the impact of culture on pregnancy and childbirth.
- To analyze abortion from a psychosocial perspective, including the legal context of abortion, the incidence of legal abortions, and the psychosocial impact of abortion.

Step Three: Take the Pre-Test

Answer these true/false questions before you read the chapter. The pages where material is discussed are indicated in the parentheses after each question. Use your performance as a guide to areas where you need to read carefully. The Answer Key for the pre-test can be found at the end of the study guide.

_____1.	The biochemical basis of genetic information is the DNA molecule. (p. 93)

_____2.	People who have the same phenotype also have the same genotype. (p. 94)

_____3.	If the gene for blue eyes is recessive and a child has blue eyes then the genotype must be homozygous for blue eyes. (p. 94)

_____4.	Most of the sex-linked genes are on the Y chromosome. (p. 95)

_____5.	Research using insects and mice shows that when the longest lived members of a species are bred the offspring have a longer than average longevity. (p. 96)

_____6.	Most significant human characteristics, such as height and intelligence, are controlled by the combined action of many genes rather than by a single gene. (p. 96)

_____7.	Approximately 15-20% of recognized pregnancies end in a first term spontaneous abortion. (p. 97)

_____8.	There are no genetic diseases that are a result of dominant genes. (p. 97)

_____9.	Once a sperm cell penetrates the membrane of an ovum, other sperm cells are locked out. (p. 101)

_____10.	No matter how much they look alike, a brother and a sister are never identical twins. (p. 102)

_____11.	Parents of children conceived through assisted reproductive technologies are more stressed and show less warmth toward their children than do parents of naturally conceived children. (p. 103)

_____12.	The alternative form of fertilization called *in vivo fertilization* requires the involvement of a second woman whose uterus is used as the initial fertilization environment. (pp. 104-105)

_____13.	The most vulnerable period in fetal development is the first two weeks when the embryo is highly susceptible to the disruptive effects of teratogens. (p. 105-107)

_____14.	Ultrasound is used to date a pregnancy more precisely. (p. 110)

____15.   It is impossible for the fetus to detect auditory stimulation in utero. (p. 111)

____16.   Infant mortality rates in the United States are about the same from one part of the country to another. (p. 114)

____17.   Infants born to depressed mothers show a depressed interpersonal style themselves. (p. 116)

____18.   Today's fathers are less likely to participate in their child's birth than fathers of the 1970s. (p. 117-118)

____19.   More babies are born to women aged 40 to 44 today than was the case in the 1960s. (pp. 118-119)

____20.   Babies born to women who smoke during pregnancy weigh less and are less responsive than babies born to mothers who do not smoke during pregnancy. (p. 120)

____21.   There is no evidence to support the fear that anesthetics used during childbirth interfere with the newborn's adaptive functioning. (p. 121)

____22.   Some of the negative effects of prenatal malnutrition can be offset after birth if the infant has access to an adequate diet. (pp. 122-123)

____23.   Most cultures view childbirth as a natural event that requires little in the way of special attention or ceremony. (p. 125)

____24.   Under current federal law, a woman must have the consent of a child's father before having an abortion. (p. 127)

____25.   Since reaching a high of 1.6 million annual abortions in the U. S. in 1990, the number of abortions has remained the same. (p. 127)

Step Four: Read Chapter 5: The Period of Pregnancy and Prenatal Development

Step Five: Review Basic Concepts by Matching Each Term and Its Definition

a. abortion   b. allele
c. artificial insemination   d. chromosome
e. genotype   f. phenotype
g. infant mortality rate   h. gestational age
i   teratogen   j. sex-linked traits
k. reaction range   l. solicitude

1.   _____   Infant deaths per 1000 live births.

2.   _____   Fertilization by medical injection of sperm.

3. _____ Genetic characteristics, the genes for which are carried on the 23rd pair of chromosomes.

4. _____ Termination of pregnancy before the fetus is able to survive outside the uterus.

5. _____ The length of time since conception.

6. _____ The hereditary information contained in the cells.

7. _____ One of the long thin strands of DNA found in the cell nucleus that carries genetic information.

8. _____ Any agent that can produce a malformation in the developing fetus.

9. _____ An attitude of care, interest, and helpfulness toward a pregnant woman.

10. _____ Observable characteristics that result from the expression of a particular genotype in a specific environment.

11. _____ Alternative states of a gene on the two paired chromosomes.

12. _____ The variety of possible expressions of genetic information depending on the environmental conditions.

Step Six: Answer the Focusing Questions

1. How is genetic information passed from parents on to their children? (pp. 92-96)

2. Explain the three ways genetic information contributes to individual differences. (pp. 96-98)

3. How does the concept of a reaction range help explain how heredity and environment interact to produce observed behavior? (pp. 100-101)

4. What are the three major developmental milestones in each of the three trimesters of the prenatal period? (pp. 103-111)

5. Choose three *teratogens* and discuss how they influence the fetus. (p. 106)

6. Explain ways fathers can be involved during pregnancy and childbirth. (pp. 116-117)

7. Does the psychosocial impact of abortion vary for women and men? What new questions were raised in your mind as you read this section? (p. 128-132)

Step Seven: Take the Post-Test

1. The human cell contains _____ pairs of chromosomes. (p. 93)
    a. 23
    b. 46
    c. 1
    d. 2

2. _____ comprise the make-up of genes. (p. 93)
    a. Segments of DNA
    b. Hundreds of chromosomes
    c. Y cells
    d. Sex cells

3. The alternate states of a gene on the two chromosome pairs are called _____. (p. 93)
    a. gametes
    b. genotypes
    c. alleles
    d. homozygous

4. The more similar two people are genetically, then the more similar they will be with respect to
    _____. (pp. 93-101)
    a. height
    b. intelligence
    c. temperament
    d. all of these

5. The genetic information about a trait is the _____; the observed trait is the _____.
    (p. 94)
    a. dominance; co-dominance
    b. phenotype; genotype
    c. allele; chromosome
    d. genotype; phenotype

6. What does it mean to say that hemophilia is a sex-linked trait? (p. 95)
    a. The disease can only be observed in men.
    b. The disease is associated with abnormal sexual behavior.
    c. The gene for the trait is carried on the 23rd pair of chromosomes.
    d. The gene for the trait is recessive.

7. How is the mapping of the human genome related to genetic counseling? (p. 98)
    a. Once the location of a genetic disease is identified, couples can be tested to see if either
        partner carries the gene.
    b. It allows people with a certain genetic disease to be paired with a partner who does not
        have the disease.
    c. It helps explain why genetic diseases are more likely in certain ethnic subgroups than in
        others.
    d. It gives the counselor more authority to decide if a couple should have a child or not.

8. When thinking about observed characteristics such as intelligence, temperament, or sociability, genetics is thought to establish the upper and lower limits possible for the expression of the trait, while the environmental conditions determine where along this continuum the behavior is actually observed. This concept is referred to as the _____. (pp. 99-101)
   a. phenotype
   b. viability factor
   c. sensitive period
   d. reaction range

9. Samantha and Samuel are brother and sister who were born three years apart. Lyle and Kyle are fraternal twins. Which set of siblings is genetically more similar? (pp. 101-102)
   a. Samantha and Samuel are more similar.
   b. Lyle and Kyle are more similar.
   c. Both sets of siblings are equally similar.
   d. More information is needed to answer this correctly.

10. The three phases of prenatal development, in order, are _____. (pp. 103-110)
   a. zygote, embryo, and fetus
   b. ovum, blastocyst, zygote
   c. first, second, and third
   d. zygote, fetus, and embryo

11. Which organ of the developing fetus is vulnerable to the negative effects of teratogens for the longest period of time? (pp. 103-110)
   a. the heart
   b. the eyes
   c. the arms and legs
   d. the central nervous system

12. The beliefs, values, and practices associated with pregnancy and childbirth are known as the _____. (pp. 103-110)
   a. infant mortality rate
   b. reaction range
   c. birth rate
   d. birth culture

13. Which of the following is NOT an alternative means of reproduction used in cases of infertility? (pp. 104-105; 110)
   a. gamete intrafallopian transfer
   b. in vivo fertilization
   c. amniocentesis
   d. artificial insemination

14. The age of viability occurs sometime between _____. (pp. 109-110)
   a. 19 and 28 weeks
   b. 28 and 36 weeks
   c. 22 and 26 weeks
   d. 24 and 32 weeks

15. Which of the following statements about infant mortality in the U.S. is most accurate? (pp. 113-114)
   a. The U.S. has the lowest infant mortality rate of the 20 leading industrialized countries in the world.
   b. The region with the lowest infant mortality rate is Washington, D.C., because it is the nation's capitol and has access to more resources than other communities.
   c. Poverty is associated with high infant mortality rates.
   d. Infant mortality rates in the U.S. are the same for black and white babies.

16. Which of the following is an example of how the developing fetus influences the pregnant woman? (pp. 114-116)
   a. Being pregnant usually has a calming, reassuring effect on a woman's emotional state.
   b. Women who are anxious about their pregnancy are likely to request more obstetrical anesthetics during labor.
   c. Being pregnant may change a woman's social status.
   d. Pregnant women who smoke cigarettes have babies with low birth weight.

17. What is the greatest risk factor for having a child with Down Syndrome? (pp. 118-119)
   a. smoking during pregnancy
   b. maternal age
   c. lack of adequate prenatal care
   d. a prenatal diet lacking protein

18. Which of the following symptoms is associated with fetal alcohol syndrome? (p. 120)
   a. abnormalities of the legs and arms
   b. disorders of the central nervous system
   c. irritability and a high pitched cry
   d. speech disorders

19. A drug called Thaledomide, which was prescribed by doctors in the 1960s for morning sickness, produced babies with _____. (p. 121)
   a. central nervous systems damage
   b. mental retardation
   c. gross deformities of the limbs
   d. blindness

20. A main point requiring definition in the abortion controversy is _____. (p. 127)
   a. the mother's culpability in exposing the embryo to teratogens
   b. a view that abortion is acceptable, and that one's friends also see it as acceptable
   c. the father's responsibility for the abortion decision
   d. the embryo is considered an individual and entitled to protection by the state

After completing the post-test, compare your score with your performance on the pre-test. Can you identify areas where significant new learning has taken place? If you still have questions about some sections of the chapter, read them again. Check the glossary. For additional test items, you may want to go to the Development Through Life web site found by going to http://www.psychology.wadsworth.com. If you still have questions, discuss them with your instructor.

Step Eight: Suggestions for Further Observation and Study

1. Review the case of Karen and Don. How did the realization that Don carried a genetic disease affect their family? What are the technical and ethical issues raised in this case?

2. Visit a local reproductive endocrinologist to obtain information on alternative means of reproduction and the personal, health, and financial factors associated with a decision to try these methods.

3. Find out if there are any genetic disease(s) that are likely to occur in your ethnic subgroup. Select a genetic disease, such as Tay Sachs disease, sickle cell anemia, or some other condition that is especially likely to occur in your ethnic subgroup, and find out more information about diagnosis, treatment, and future prevention of that disease.

4. Visit a local public health facility or interview an obstetrician about the transmission of AIDS from mother-to-child. Discuss outcomes and treatments for children born to mothers with AIDS.

5. Visit a planned parenthood center in your community. Speak to the director or program coordinator about the types of services and programs provided by the center. What problems does the center face in serving its target population? How does the center evaluate its contribution to healthy pregnancies and low infant mortality rates in your community?

6. Learning through Technology: InfoTrac®
    For further study, explore InfoTrac® College Edition, an online library. Go to http://www.infotrac-college.com and use the pass code that came on the card with your book. To learn more, look up the following search terms and subdivisions in InfoTrac®.

PREGNANCY
    Nutrition in Pregnancy
    Morning Sickness
    Pregnancy, Multiple
    Alcoholism in Pregnancy
    Smoking in Pregnancy
    HIV Infection in Pregnancy
    AIDS in Pregnancy

HUMAN REPRODUCTIVE
    TECHNOLOGY
    Moral and Ethical Principal
    Laws and Regulations
    Genetic Aspects
    Artificial Insemination
    Surrogate Motherhood

CHILDBIRTH
    Couvade
    Planning
    Technique
    Complications
    Childbirth at Home

GENETIC DISORDERS
    Genetic Defects
    Genetic Diseases
    Genetic Diagnosis
    Amniocentesis

ABORTION

CHAPTER SIX
Infancy (First 24 Months)

Step One: Review the Chapter Outline

Newborns
Developmental Tasks
 The Development of Sensory/Perceptual and Motor Functions
 Case Study: The Cotton Family
  Attachment
  Sensorimotor Intelligence and Early Causal Schemes
  Understanding the Nature of Objects and Creating Categories
  Emotional Development
The Psychosocial Crisis: Trust versus Mistrust
 Trust
 Mistrust
The Central Process for Resolving the Crisis: Mutuality with the Caregiver
 Coordination, Mismatch, and Repair of Interactions
 Establishing a Functional Rhythm in the Family
 Parents with Psychological Problems
The Prime Adaptive Ego Quality and the Core Pathology
 Hope
 Withdrawal
Applied Topic: The Role of Parents
 Safety in the Physical Environment
 Fostering Emotional and Cognitive Development
 Fathers' and Mothers' Parental Behavior
 Parents as Advocates
 The Importance of Social Support
Chapter Summary

Step Two: Review the Chapter Objectives

- To identify important milestones in the maturation of the sensory and motor systems, and to describe the interactions among these systems during the first two years of life.
- To define social attachment as the process through which infants develop strong emotional bonds with others, and to describe the dynamics of attachment formation during infancy.
- To describe the development of sensorimotor intelligence, including an analysis of how infants organize experiences and conceptualize causality.
- To examine how infants understand the properties of objects, including the sense that objects are permanent, that they have unique properties and functions, and that they can be categorized.
- To examine the nature of emotional development, including emotional differentiation, the interpretation of emotions, and emotional regulation.
- To analyze the factors that contribute to the resolution of the psychosocial crisis of trust versus mistrust, including the achievement of mutuality with the caregiver and the attainment of a sense of hope or withdrawal.

- To evaluate the critical role of parents/caregivers during infancy with special attention to issues of safety in the physical environment; optimizing cognitive, social, and emotional development; and the role of parents/caregivers as advocates for their infants with other agencies and systems.

Step Three: Take the Pre-Test

Answer these true/false questions before you read the chapter. The pages where material is discussed are indicated in the parentheses after each question. Use your performance as a guide to areas where you need to read carefully. The Answer Key for the pre-test can be found at the end of the study guide.

____1.   Babies naturally know how to crawl. They do it without practice as soon as you put them down on the floor. (pp. 142-143)

____2.   Babies cannot hear in utero. (p. 139)

____3.   Newborns can differentiate sweet, sour, bitter, and salty tastes. (p.142)

____4.   A normative sequence of motor development is grasping, sitting, crawling, walking, and standing. (pp. 143-145)

____5.   A child's threshold for arousal which could be evidenced at the psychological, emotional, or motor level is called reactive-regulation. (p. 147)

____6.   A child's self-regulator capacities, or behavioral inhibition, may range from bold or brazen to inhibited and cautious. (pp. 147-148)

____7.   Children react differently in a variety of situations, thus revealing that child temperament is a complex picture of the interaction of child and environmental characteristics. (p. 146)

____8.   The ability to crawl has no relevance to the development of attachment. (pp. 149-150)

____9.   Stranger anxiety is considered to be a normal developmental behavior that demonstrates a child's growing preference for the object of attachment. (pp. 150-151)

____10.   Once an attachment has been formed, children become less and less comfortable about separating from the object of attachment. (p. 151)

____11.   In the United States, about two-thirds of the mother-infant dyads who have been evaluated in the Strange Situation show evidence of an anxious-avoidant attachment. (p. 153)

____12.   The exploratory behavior of babies who show an anxious-resistant attachment is noticeably disrupted by the caregiver's departure. (p. 153)

____13.   The kinds and quality of relationships in the first six months of life have no relevance in the formation of attachments. (pp. 154-155)

____14.   Cross-cultural research on infant attachment supports that there is little variation in parent-child interactions across racial and ethnic groups. (p. 155)

_____15.　　　According to Piaget, reflexes are the built-in, genetic origins of intelligence. (p. 157)

_____16.　　　Categorization requires the ability to name objects. (p. 160)

_____17.　　　According to Piaget, sensorimotor adaptation is the chief mechanism governing the growth of intelligence during infancy. (p. 157)

_____18.　　　Adults have measurable emotional reactions to infant crying including changes in heart rate and breathing which indicate that the cry serves as a stressor. (pp. 161-163)

_____19.　　　In the first 2 years of life, infants have states of arousal but no true expression of emotions. (pp. 161-163)

_____20.　　　Emotions provide a way for adults to assess an infant's inner state. (pp. 161-163)

_____21.　　　One way newborns reduce the intensity of distress is by turning their heads away. (pp. 163-164)

_____22.　　　Infant reflexes, such as the startle response provide a biological basis for mistrust. (p. 165)

_____23.　　　In normal mother-infant dyads, communication becomes increasingly mismatched as the baby matures. (p. 169)

_____24.　　　In the intervention study that focused on distressed mother-infant dyads at risk for attachment disturbances, it was found that it was not possible to repair these attachment relationships. (p. 172)

_____25.　　　Fathers tend to view their infants as less cognitively and socially competent than mothers do. (pp. 176-177)

Step Four: Read Chapter 6: Infancy

Step Five: Review Basic Concepts By Matching Each Term and Its Definition

a.	critical period	b.	mistrust
c.	mutuality	d.	object permanence
e.	sensorimotor intelligence	f.	separation anxiety
g.	social attachment	h.	synchrony
i.	temperament	j.	trust
k.	emotional regulation	l.	intersubjectivity

1.　　_____　　Strategies for dealing with intense emotions.

2.　　_____　　Rhythmic, well-timed, appropriately responsive interactions.

3.　　_____　　A time of maximum sensitivity to or readiness for the development of a particular skill or behavior pattern.

4. _____ A strong, affectionate bond that develops between infants and their caregivers.

5. _____ The ability of two people to meet each other's needs and share each other's concerns and feelings.

6. _____ Feelings of fear or sadness associated with the departure of the attachment figure.

7. _____ An emotional sense that the environment is capable of meeting one's basic needs and that one is worthy of the love of others.

8. _____ Relatively stable characteristics of response to environmental stimuli, largely under genetic control.

9. _____ The ability of two or more people to know what one another is experiencing.

10. _____ A sense of unpredictability in the environment and suspicion about one's own worth or doubt that one's needs will be met.

11. _____ A scheme acquired during the sensorimotor stage of development in which infants become aware that an object continues to exist even when it is hidden or moved from place to place.

12. _____ In Piaget's theory of development, the first stage of cognitive growth during which schema are established on the basis of sensory and motor experiences.

Step Six: Answer the Focusing Questions

1. List the major competencies in each of the following domains of the sensory/perceptual system that occur during the first few months of life: hearing, vision, taste and smell, and touch. (p. 137-142)

2. List and describe the five sequential stages in the development of social attachment. (p. 148)

3. List the four patterns of attachment. Describe the behaviors that are characteristic of the infant and the parenting behaviors that are likely to lead to the development of each pattern. (p. 153-154)

4. Describe sensorimotor intelligence and define each of the six phases in the development of causal schemes. (pp. 157-158)

5. Describe how researchers study object permanence. Why is this considered an important concept to study? (pp. 159-160)

6. Distinguish the differences in differentiation, interpretation, and regulation of emotion during infancy. (pp. 161-166)

7. Describe the development of trust and mistrust in infancy. How might each of these orientations affect development in later stages? (pp. 167-168)

8.   How do infants and caregivers achieve mutuality in their interactions? (pp. 168-169)

9.   Trace how the development of a sense of trust leads to the prime adaptive ego quality of hope. How does the worldview of hope affect later development? How does hope affect your life? Do the same kind of analysis for mistrust and withdrawal. (pp. 171-174)

10.   What do you think are the most important things parents can do to foster optimal development in their infants? (p. 174-178)

Step Seven: Take the Post-Test

1.   Sensory experiences can strengthen certain neural pathways in the infant brain while less used pathways may disappear. This is called _____. (p. 139)
       a.   habituation
       b.   plasticity
       c.   visual acuity
       d.   intersubjectivity

2.   Which of the following sensory/motor systems is least well developed in newborns? (p. 143)
       a.   taste
       b.   voluntary motor activity
       c.   vision
       d.   hearing

3.	Which of the following motor skills is NOT acquired during the first year of life? (p. 145)
	a.	standing alone
	b.	running
	c.	rolling over
	d.	crawling

4.	Infants who are inactive and have mild, low-key reactions to new environmental stimuli, are generally negative in mood, and have a hard time adjusting to new situations are considered to fall within which temperament category? (pp. 146-147)
	a.	insecure
	b.	difficult
	c.	secure
	d.	slow-to-warm-up

5.	During the second half of the first year two signs of a child's growing attachment to a specific other person are _____. (pp. 150-151)
	a.	first habits and circular reactions
	b.	stranger anxiety and separation anxiety
	c.	rooting and grasping
	d.	intersubjectivity and matching

6.	One-year old Benjamin often returns to his father repeatedly for a hug when playing with his trucks on the family room floor. Returning to his father shows that Benjamin is using his father as a_____. (pp. 152-153)
	a.	habituation point
	b.	exploration point
	c.	secure base
	d.	behavioral base

7.	Which of the following is used as evidence that an attachment has been formed? (pp. 152-153)
	a.	An infant calls to his or her attachment figure by name.
	b.	An infant tries to maintain physical contact with the object of attachment.
	c.	An infant acts fussier in the afternoons than in the evenings.
	d.	An infant shows distress when the loved person comes near.

8.	Corey actively explores the living room at his aunt's house while his mother is sitting on the couch. When she leaves to get a drink in the kitchen, Corey fusses, but he calms down quickly as soon as she returns. Corey may be best described as having a (n) _____ attachment. (p. 153)
	a.	disorganized
	b.	anxious-avoidant
	c.	secure
	d.	anxious-resistant

9.	According to Piaget's theory, what is the primary mechanism underlying the growth of intelligence during infancy? (p. 157)
	a.	synchrony
	b.	sensorimotor adaptation
	c.	assimilation
	d.	intersubjectivity

10.   The first phase in the development of causal schemes is the phase of _____. (p. 158)
       a.   insight
       b.   circular reactions
       c.   reflexes
       d.   smiling

11.   Which of the following is an example of sensorimotor intelligence? (p. 157)
       a.   sucking differently from a bottle and from a breast
       b.   solving an arithmetic problem
       c.   pretending to be a fireman
       d.   using words as labels for objects

12.   Ricky, who is 6 months old, discovers that if he lets his spoon drop it will fall to the floor and make a noise. He repeatedly drops his spoon and expresses great delight. This behavior is an example of _____. (p. 157)
       a.   sensorimotor causality
       b.   attachment
       c.   object permanence
       d.   imprinting

13.   Which of the following is among the earliest emotions to be expressed in infancy, before 6 months of age? (p. 161)
       a.   pleasure
       b.   pride
       c.   defiance
       d.   guilt

14.   _____ illustrates how members of a cultural group build a shared view of reality during infancy. (p. 166)
       a.   Intersubjectivity
       b.   Social referencing
       c.   Attachment
       d.   None of these

15.   In infancy trust refers to the infant's sense that he or she is _____. (p. 167)
       a.   creative
       b.   intelligent
       c.   valued
       d.   skillful and resourceful

16.   Mistrust may develop if a caregiver is unusually harsh while meeting an infant's needs or if _____. (pp. 167-168)
       a.   the caregiver responds too quickly
       b.   the caregiver talks to the infant too much
       c.   the caregiver caters to the child's every whim
       d.   the caregiver cannot identify the child's needs and respond appropriately to them

17. Which of the following is the central process for resolving the psychosocial crisis of infancy? (p. 168)
    a. education
    b. social support
    c. mutuality with the caregiver
    d. imitation

18. A critical period refers to which of the following? (pp. 168-169)
    a. a time of intense interaction between parents and babies
    b. a life stage that is more important than other life stages
    c. a time of maximal readiness for the development of some behavior
    d. a time in life when a person has to make an important life decision

19. Within the process of communication the pattern of coordination, mismatch, and repair builds a sense of _____ between the infant and the caregiver. (p. 169)
    a. mistrust
    b. causality
    c. anxiety
    d. mutuality

20. In their parental roles, mothers in the United States tend to emphasize _____ while fathers tend to emphasize _____. (pp. 176-177)
    a. physical play; caregiving
    b. the process of development; product
    c. object permanence; the development of causal schemes
    d. intersubjectivity; communication repair

After completing the post-test, compare your score with your performance on the pre-test. Can you identify areas where significant new learning has taken place? If you still have questions about some sections of the chapter, read them again. Check the glossary. For additional test items, you may want to go to the *Development Through Life* web site found by going to http://www.psychology.wadsworth.com. If you still have questions, discuss them with your instructor.

Step Eight: Suggestions for Further Observation and Study

1. Visit the newborn nursery of a hospital and watch the babies for half an hour. Keep an observation log of what you observe. Can you detect individual differences in responsiveness, activity level, or irritability? Do you notice babies starting to cry in response to the crying of other babies?

2. Interview a parent who gave birth to a premature infant who was a very-low-birth-weight baby. Discuss with them the difficulties of caring for such a small child and the health difficulties their child may or may not be suffering from.

3. Construct a collage showing differences in infants' smiles. Make sure to show a wide range of children of varied ages. Discuss the differences and the wide variety of meanings that can be produced in response to many stimuli.

4.   Review recent literature on the impact of day care or alternative child care arrangements on development during infancy. Develop a list of recommendations about infant child care that parents could use when considering whether to place an infant in child care and what the best kind of arrangement would be.

5.   Ask some adults, adolescents, and young children what trust and mistrust mean to them. Ask them to describe to you how they know when they can trust someone or when they cannot. How does the use of these terms differ for the three different age levels? How do the popular uses of these words compare to the psychosocial meanings discussed in the text?

6.   Imagine that you are responsible for the care of an infant where you currently live. What are the potential risks and hazards of your home environment for the infant? What steps would you take to reduce risks and increase the baby's safety in your home? As you think about this, do you prefer the strategy of restricting the baby to keep her or him safe, or the strategy of altering the environment to permit maximum exploration?

7.   Learning through Technology: InfoTrac®
For further study, explore InfoTrac® College Edition, an online library. Go to http://www.infotrac-college.com and use the pass code that came on the card with your book. To learn more, look up the following search terms and subdivisions in InfoTrac®.

INFANTS

REFLEXES

MOTOR DEVELOPMENT

APGAR SCORE

TEMPERAMENT IN CHILDREN

EMOTIONS IN INFANTS

ATTACHMENT BEHAVIOR
    Measurement
    Psychological Aspects
    Imprinting
    Attachment Behavior in
    Children

CHAPTER SEVEN
Toddlerhood (2-3 Years)

Step One: Review the Chapter Outline

Case Study: Alice Walker Goes to the Fair
Developmental Tasks
    Elaboration of Locomotion
    Language Development
    Fantasy Play
    Self-Control
Connecting Theory and Research to Life: The Control of Anger Feelings
The Psychosocial Crisis: Autonomy versus Shame and Doubt
    Autonomy
    Shame and Doubt
The Central Process: Imitation
The Prime Adaptive Ego Quality and The Core Pathology
    Will
    Compulsion
The Impact of Poverty on Psychosocial Development in Toddlerhood
Applied Topic: Child Care
    Intelligence and Academic Achievement
    Social Competence
    Peer Relations
    Directions for the Future
Chapter Summary

Step Two: Review the Chapter Objectives

- To describe the expansion of motor skills during toddlerhood, indicating their importance for the child's expanding capacity to explore the environment and experience opportunities for mastery.
- To document accomplishments in language development and describe the major influence of interactive experiences and the language environment for the process of language acquisition.
- To examine the development of fantasy play and its importance for cognitive and social development.
- To examine the development of self-control, especially impulse management and goal attainment, highlighting strategies young children use to help them regulate their actions.
- To analyze the psychosocial crisis of autonomy versus shame and doubt, to clarify the central process of imitation, and to describe the prime adaptive ego strength of will and the core pathology of compulsion.
- To conceptualize the impact of poverty on development in toddlerhood.
- To apply a psychosocial analysis to the topic of child care, emphasizing the impact of the nature and quality of care on development during toddlerhood.

Step Three: Take the Pre-Test

Answer these true/false questions before you read the chapter. The pages where material is discussed are indicated in the parentheses after each question. Use your performance as a guide to areas where you need to read carefully. The Answer Key for the pre-test can be found at the end of the study guide.

____1. To the extent that coping involves the ability to maintain freedom of movement under conditions of threat, the locomotor skills acquired during toddlerhood provide a fundamental group of lifelong strategies for "fight" or "flight." (pp. 183-184)

____2. Even at the beginning of running, toddler running is very similar to adult running. (pp. 184-185)

____3. Representational skills allow children to share their experiences with other people and to create experiences they imagine. (p. 185)

____4. Communicative competence begins during toddlerhood and is completed by the end of this stage. (p. 185)

____5. During toddlerhood, children learn to recognize symbols and signs. (p. 185)

____6. Research on cognitive development suggests that gains in the capacity for symbolic thought do not influence subsequent intellectual development. (pp. 185-186)

____7. The only linguistic accomplishment of infancy is babbling. (pp. 188-189)

____8. The ability to understand words precedes the ability to produce spoken words and phrases. (pp. 188-189)

____9. Children in all cultures use the same first two-word combinations. (pp. 188-189)

____10. The fundamentals of language are well established by age 4, with children being able to structure their sentences using most of the rules of grammar without having had direct instruction. (p. 191)

____11. Adults may assume that toddlers fully understand the more abstract meanings of the words they use, but in fact children may not fully understand the meaning of the words they use. (pp. 192-194)

____12. Evidence suggests that young bilingual children have difficulty knowing when to use one language and when to use the other. (p. 194)

____13. Children's use of words to refer to feelings and to describe emotions increases notably at 3 and 4 years of age. (pp. 196-197)

____14. The difference between make-believe and reality can become blurred for children but not for adults. (p. 197)

____15. Pretending to drive a car is an example of sensorimotor play. (p. 197)

____16.   Children who have had many changes in their child-care arrangements are more likely to engage in complex social pretend play with other children than children who have not had many changes in their child-care arrangements. (pp. 198-200)

____17.   Research suggests that very few toddlers have imaginary companions and that those who do show evidence of less advanced abilities in other forms of symbolic play. (pp. 201-202)

____18.   Infants have a variety of strategies for soothing themselves and reducing stimulation. (pp. 202-203)

____19.   Language skills interfere with impulse control and self-directed goal attainment. (p. 202)

____20.   There is no point trying to teach toddlers to control their angry feelings because they are unable to empathize with the distress of others. (p. 203)

____21.   Discipline should not be immediate; parents should handle it later after thinking it over. (pp. 204-205)

____22.   Will is commonly associated with toddlerhood; actually few normal toddlers develop this prime adaptive ego quality. (p. 211)

____23.   Even if they have not done anything wrong, some children will feel shame when they believe their behavior has not met the standards of their ego ideal. (p. 208)

____24.   The highest percentage of non-parental care is center-based care (31%). (p. 214)

____25.   The United States is one of the leaders among industrialized nations in the formation of a national child-care policy. (pp. 217-218)

Step Four: Read Chapter 7: Toddlerhood (Ages 2 and 3)

Step Five: Review Basic Concepts By Matching Each Term and Its Definition

a.   autonomy
b.   communicative competence
c.   discipline
d.   imitation
e.   induction
f.   love withdrawal
g.   power assertion
h.   preoperational thought
i.   self-control
j.   shame
k.   scaffolding
l.   symbolic play

1.   _____   The ability to use all aspects of language in order to produce and interpret communication.

2.   _____   Explanations that point out the consequences of a behavior for others.

3.   _____   In Piaget's theory of cognitive development, the stage during which representational skills are acquired.

4. _____ The ability to restrain impulses and the ability to function as a causal agent.

5. _____ The ability to do things on one's own.

6. _____ Strategies for punishing or changing behavior.

7. _____ The creation of pretend characters, objects, and situations in play.

8. _____ Repetitions of another person's words, gestures, or actions.

9. _____ The process through which an adult and child arrive at a shared understanding, and then the adult interacts so as to expand the child's communicative competence.

10. _____ A discipline technique in which a parent's size and strength are used to dominate a child.

11. _____ An emotional response to being discovered doing something wrong.

12. _____ A discipline technique in which a child's behavior can result in loss of parental affection.

Step Six: Answer the Focusing Questions

1. List the significant achievements in the toddler's capacity for locomotion. (p. 183-185)

2. Define semiotic or representational thinking. What are some examples? (p. 185)

3. Detail the process of language development. (pp. 185-197)

4.   List and describe the four dimensions of fantasy play during toddlerhood. (pp. 197-202)

5.   Describe factors that contribute to a toddler's growing ability to exercise self-control. What are factors that interfere with this ability? (pp. 202-206)

6.   How might different discipline techniques contribute to the resolution of the psychosocial crisis of autonomy versus shame and doubt? (pp. 208-210)

7.   Detail how poverty influences a toddler's biopsychosocial development. (pp. 212-214)

8.   What is the quality of child care in the United States? What are the psychosocial needs of toddlers and how are they reflected or not reflected in America's child care settings? (pp. 214-218)

Step Seven: Take the Post-Test

1.   The developmental task of _____ plays a central role in toddler's psychosocial development by transforming ideas into action and prompting interactions. (pp. 183-184)
        a.   locomotion
        b.   communication
        c.   generation
        d.   all of these

2.   _____ is a string of consonants and vowels, which begins around 6 months of age. (p. 188)
        a.   Cooing
        b.   Chattering
        c.   Talking
        d.   Babbling

3.   The ability to understand words, called _____, develops ahead of the ability to produce spoken words and language. (p. 189)
        a.   receptive language
        b.   productive language
        c.   referential language
        d.   interpretive language

4.   What is the meaning of the term *holophase*? (p. 189)
        a.   grammatical transformations
        b.   two-word sentences
        c.   vocalization without meaning
        d.   single word utterances accompanied by gestures, action, vocal intonation, and emotion

5.   Quickly grasping the meaning of a word within context of a conversation is called _____. (p. 190)
        a.   expansion
        b.   prompting
        c.   fast-mapping
        d.   none of these

6.   A major accomplishment in language development during the second year of life is the child's ability to _____. (p. 190)
        a.   form two-word sentences
        b.   vocalize
        c.   babble
        d.   use the grammatically correct form of singular, possessive pronouns

7.   How does a parent's use of expansion help a child develop communication skills? (p. 195)
        a.   It elaborates on the child's expression.
        b.   It avoids forcing the child to speak.
        c.   It urges the child to listen more carefully.
        d.   It moves to a level of greater abstraction.

8. Billy says "Go Bye Bye," and his Mother responds "Yes Mommy is going Bye Bye, I am going to work Billy." This is an example of: _____. (p. 195)
   a. prompting
   b. expansion
   c. development
   d. bootstrapping

9. Which of the following is an example of symbolic play? (p. 197)
   a. playing the drums
   b. playing with a rattle
   c. playing house
   d. playing with one's toes

10. Which of the following is an example of preoperational thought? (p. 197)
    a. throwing a ball
    b. playing cards
    c. pretending to be a superhero
    d. crying

11. Which of the following characteristics is associated with well-developed fantasy play skills? (pp. 197-198)
    a. flexible problem solving skills
    b. social isolation
    c. poor verbal communication skills
    d. daydreaming and inability to focus

12. Which of the following is NOT a strategy that toddlers use to achieve self-control? (p. 202)
    a. diverting their attention to something else
    b. talking to themselves
    c. insisting on having their own way
    d. creating an imaginary situation in which disturbing problems can be expressed and resolved

13. One of the important elements of self-control that develops during toddlerhood is the ability to _____. (p. 202)
    a. regress to an earlier form of impulse gratification
    b. feel out of control
    c. delay the gratification or expression of impulses
    d. express impulses quickly

14. "Mommy doesn't love you when you do that," is an example of which discipline practice? (p. 205)
    a. power assertion
    b. love withdrawal
    c. alienation
    d. inductions

15. Which of the following is a form of discipline in which the caregiver points out the consequences of a certain behavior and redirects the child's behavior? (p. 205)
    a.   love withdrawal
    b.   induction
    c.   power assertion
    d.   time out

16. The negative resolution of the psychosocial crisis of toddlerhood is _____. (p. 208)
    a.   autonomy
    b.   independence
    c.   shame and doubt
    d.   alienation

17. Which of the following is an example of autonomy? (p. 208)
    a.   Nobody likes me.
    b.   I hate you.
    c.   That's not fair.
    d.   I can do it myself.

18. The central process of toddlerhood, which fosters the emergence of autonomy is _____. (p. 208)
    a.   shame
    b.   doubt
    c.   imitation
    d.   none of these

19. Which of the following has been documented as a positive consequence of participation in quality day care? (p. 216)
    a.   improved memorization skills
    b.   higher IQ scores in adolescence and adulthood
    c.   higher levels of social competence, self-esteem, and empathy
    d.   better chances of receiving a college scholarship

20. Which of the statements about the impact of day care is false? (pp. 216-218)
    a.   Children who have had quality day care experiences tend to show higher levels of empathy.
    b.   Children who have had quality day care experiences are less compliant with their parents.
    c.   Children who have been in the same day care center for a long period of time develop more complex peer play skills.
    d.   Children who have had quality day care experiences are more likely to play alone and to be described as shy.

After completing the post-test, compare your score with your performance on the pre-test. Can you identify areas where significant new learning has taken place? If you still have questions about some sections of the chapter, read them again. Check the glossary. For additional test items, you may want to go to the *Development Through Life* web site found by going to http://www.psychology.wadsworth.com. If you still have questions, discuss them with your instructor.

Step Eight: Suggestions for Further Observation and Study

1.   What can you recall about the nature of your own fantasy play when you were a toddler? Ask your parents or older siblings what they can remember. What kinds of pretense did you enjoy? What sorts of characters or situations did you create? Did you have some special props or toys that were central to your pretense? Who were your play companions and what kinds of group fantasy activities did you create?

2.   Ask a 2 ½ or 3 year old to explain a game to you or to tell you how a toy works. What special qualities do you notice about this child's use of language?

3.   Read the advice to parents about discipline that is provided in two or three parenting books available in your local bookstore. How does that advice compare to the research evidence on discipline techniques discussed in the text?

4.   Visit a child care center. Watch the children at play. What kinds of experiences seem to contribute to autonomy in this setting? What factors might interfere with autonomy or produce feelings of shame and doubt?

5.   Learning through Technology: InfoTrac®
      For further study, explore InfoTrac® College Edition, an online library. Go to http://www.infotrac-college.com and use the pass code that came on the card with your book. To learn more, look up the following search terms and subdivisions in InfoTrac®.

TODDLERS
    Behavior
    Psychology and Mental Health

LANGUAGE ACQUISITION
    Analysis
    Parent Participation
    PET Imaging
    Research

SECOND LANGUAGE
    ACQUISITION and/or
    BILINGUALISM
    Political Aspects
    Psychological Aspects
    Bilingual Education

PRETEND PLAY

ANGER IN CHILDREN

DAY CARE CENTERS
    Evaluation
    Research
    Social Aspects
    Services

POVERTY
    Measurement
    Prevention
    Psychological Aspects
    United States

TOYS
    History
    Psychological Aspects
    Safety and Security Measures

TOILET TRAINING

CHAPTER EIGHT
Early School Age (4-6 years)

Step One: Review the Chapter Outline

Developmental Tasks
    Gender Identification
Case Study: Gender Identification in Early Childhood
    Early Moral Development
Case Study: Early Learning About Obedience
    Self-Theory
    Peer Play
The Psychosocial Crisis: Initiative versus Guilt
    Initiative
    Guilt
The Central Process: Identification
The Prime Adaptive Ego Quality and the Core Pathology
    Purpose
    Inhibition
Applied Topic: School Readiness
    Defining Readiness
    Measuring Kindergarten Readiness
    Obstacles in the Way of School Readiness
    Who is Responsible for Meeting the Goal for School Readiness?
Chapter Summary

Step Two: Review the Chapter Objectives

- To describe the process of gender identification during early school age and its importance for the way a child interprets his or her experiences.
- To describe the process of early moral development, drawing from theories and research to explain how knowledge, emotion, and action combine to produce internalized morality.
- To analyze changes in the self-theory, with special focus on the Theory of Mind and self-esteem during the early school-age years.
- To explore the transition to more complex group play and the process of friendship development in the early school-age years.
- To explain the psychosocial crisis of initiative versus guilt, the central process of identification, the prime adaptive ego function of purpose, and the core pathology of inhibition.
- To analyze the construct of school readiness, its relation to the developmental tasks of early school age, and the obstacles that may prevent children from being able to adapt and learn in the school environment.

Step Three: Take the Pre-Test

Answer these true/false questions before you read the chapter. The pages where material is discussed are indicated in the parentheses after each question. Use your performance as a guide to areas where you need to read carefully. The Answer Key for the pre-test can be found at the end of the study guide.

_____1.   It is normative for 3 and 4-year-old children in the U.S. to be enrolled in some type of school of early childcare setting. (p. 222)

_____2.   Male and female brains are basically identical. No gender differences can be traced to differences in the structure or composition of the brain. (pp. 222-224)

_____3.   Gender labels are the earliest component of gender identification to be achieved. (p. 225)

_____4.   Children aged 6 and 7 are more flexible in their approach to applying gender role standards than younger children. (p. 226)

_____5.   Gender schemes are personal theories about cultural expectations and stereotypes for male and female behavior. (p. 226)

_____6.   The process of identification occurs only in childhood. After adolescence, one no longer forms identifications with others. (p. 227)

_____7.   Externalization is the earliest process of moral development. (p. 231)

_____8.   Within the framework of autonomous morality, children see rules as fixed and unchangeable. (p. 232)

_____9.   If a child has been disciplined in the past for misbehaving, a child contemplating misbehaving again should feel a state of tension or guilt. This is called avoidance conditioning. (p. 231)

_____10.   In the first stage of Kohlberg's model of moral reasoning, individuals judge a behavior based on whether the action was rewarded or punished. If a behavior is punished, then it was morally wrong. (p. 233)

_____11.   Kohlberg's levels of moral thought are a priori morality, morality, post morality. (p. 233)

_____12.   Children as young as 4 or 5 can tell the difference between a moral transgression and a transgression of social convention. (p. 233)

_____13.   Neopsychoanalytic theory or object relations theory, views the critical time for moral development as infancy rather than the early school age years. (p. 235)

_____14.   The capacity for empathy is first observed in the early-school-age period when children try to help each other. (p. 236)

_____15.   Empathy refers to the cognitive capacity to consider a situation from the point of view of another person. (p. 236)

_____16.   It is estimated that children watch nearly 30 hours of television a week. (pp. 239-241)

_____17.   Research on the impact of televised violence on young children's behaviors and beliefs is inconclusive. There is no clear evidence of its negative impact, nor is there evidence that there are any positive outcomes of this type of TV viewing. (pp. 239-241)

_____18.   Since the self-theory is based on personal experiences and observations, one would expect it to be modified over the life course by participation in new roles. (p. 243)

_____19.   The implication of the studies of contextual dissonance reported in the text is that self-esteem is bolstered by a feeling of continuity and belonging. (p. 247)

_____20.   Young's children's friendship groups tend to be segregated by sex. (p. 250)

_____21.   In peer play with friends there is very little conflict. (p. 250)

_____22.   Both boys and girls of early school age seem to enjoy dyadic (two-person) groups over larger groups. (p. 251)

_____23.   In early-school-age all-girl play groups, the interactions include frequent boasts, commands, and playful teasing. (pp. 247-250)

_____24.   A sense of initiative is an outgrowth of early experiences as children explore their social world. (p. 251)

_____25.   A sense of inhibition can emerge when parents use high levels of love withdrawal or guilt-inducing behaviors as a form of discipline. (p. 256)

Step Four: Read Chapter 8: Early School Age (4 to 6 years)

Step Five: Review Basic Concepts By Matching Each Term and Its Definition

a.	self-esteem	b.	self-theory
c.	sex-role standards	d.	gender preference
e.	empathy	f.	gender label
g.	group play	h.	guilt
i.	identification	j.	initiative
k.	perspective-taking	l.	preconventional morality

1.   _____   Active experimentation and investigation of the environment.

2.   _____   A theory that links a person's understanding of the nature of the world, the nature of the self, and the meaning of interactions between the self and the environment.

3.   _____   The capacity to recognize and experience the emotional state of another person.

4.   _____   The evaluative dimension of the self that includes feelings of worthiness, pride, and discouragement.

5.   _____   Cultural norms about the attributes that should characterize males and females.

6.   _____   A psychological mechanism in which people incorporate valued characteristics of important others.

7.   _____   A word that indicates the sex of a person.

8.   _____   An early form of games such as "Ring Around the Rosie" that has a ritualized format and few rules.

9.   _____   An emotion associated with doing something wrong or anticipating doing something wrong.

10.   _____   A positive value for being a member of one gender group or the other.

11.   _____   In Kohlberg's scheme, the first stage of moral development when judgments are based on the consequences of behavior.

12.   _____   The ability to take the point of view of another, especially when that person's point of view is different from one's own.

Step Six: Answer the Focusing Questions

1.   Detail differences between the individual differences perspective and the constructivist perspective for explaining gender differences. (pp. 224-225)

2.   List and describe the four dimensions of gender identification. Make sure to give an example of each. (pp. 225-226)

3.   How do rewards and punishments, empathy, perspective taking, moral standards, parental discipline, moral reasoning and parental identification contribute to morality during the early school-age-period? (pp. 230-241)

4.   Describe self-theory. (pp. 243-246)

5.   Define self-esteem. Why is self-esteem during the early-school-age period so vulnerable to fluctuations? (pp. 247-248)

6.   Describe how identification contributes to the resolution of the psychosocial crisis of initiative versus guilt? (pp. 254-256)

7.   Compare and contrast parents' and teachers' measures of kindergarten readiness. (pp. 257-260)

8.   Who do you believe is responsible for meeting the national goal for school readiness? Describe a program or policy initiative you would create to help prepare our nation's children for school. (pp. 259-260)

Step Seven: Take the Post-Test

1. Which is the earliest component of gender identification to be achieved? (pp. 225-226)
    a. gender-role standards
    b. gender label
    c. gender constancy
    d. gender preference

2. Some parents believe that boys should be assertive and girls should try to please others. This is an example of _____. (p. 226)
    a. a gender-role standard
    b. a gender label
    c. a gender preference
    d. none of these

3. Which of the following theories views moral behavior as a result of repeated associations between valued behavior and reinforcements? (pp. 231-232)
    a. learning theory
    b. psychoanalytic theory
    c. cognitive-developmental theory
    d. social-role theory

4. Cognitive developmental theorists and learning theorists agree that which of the following guides a very young child's moral judgments? (p. 232-233)
    a. conscience
    b. empathy
    c. rewards and punishments
    d. a sense of justice

5. When children see rules as a product of cooperative agreements, they are said to have achieved a level of _____ morality. (p. 232)
    a. schematic
    b. heteronomous
    c. autonomous
    d. overt

6. A toddler offers her own favorite cuddly blanket to her father when he hurts his leg. This is an example of which type of empathy? (pp. 236-237)
    a. empathy for another's feelings
    b. egocentric empathy
    c. empathy for another's life conditions
    d. global empathy

7. Which statement best reflects a 4 to 6 year old child's social perspective-taking ability? Early-school-age children _____. (pp. 236-237)
    a. assume that everyone involved views a situation just as they do
    b. realize that people can take each other's point of view into account before they decide to act
    c. realize that all the people involved in the situation may see it differently
    d. all of these

8.   Research indicates that one consequence for children of viewing televised violence may be
        _____. (pp. 239-241)
        a.   an increase in the child's dislike of violence
        b.   an increase in the child's repertoire of aggressive behaviors
        c.   a decrease in the child's need to be aggressive
        d.   an increase in the child's fear of his/her father

9.   Which of the following may be considered an example of how television could promote optimal
        development? (pp. 239-241)
        a.   watching television might lead to expectations that problems can be easily solved
        b.   watching television might lower a child's self-esteem
        c.   watching television might reduce a child's social interactions
        d.   watching television might help children experience empathy for others

10.   Which of the following is a consequence of watching television? (pp. 239-241)
        a.   It decreases participation in community and recreational activities.
        b.   It helps children view the world as a safe, caring place.
        c.   It increases social interaction.
        d.   It decreases interest in commercial products such as toys, candy, and cereal.

11.   The text treats the _____ as a theory that links a person's understanding about the nature
        of the world, the nature of the self, and the meaning of interactions between the self and the
        environment. (p. 243)
        a.   reward structure
        b.   gender preference
        c.   superego
        d.   self-concept

12.   William James differentiated the "I" and "me" as the components of the self. What is the "me"?
        (pp. 243-245)
        a.   the self as knower
        b.   the self that imitates behavior
        c.   the self that reflects upon its own qualities
        d.   the self as an object that can be described by others

13.   Which of the following statements about group play is most accurate? (pp. 249-250)
        a.   Group games require a referee or umpire in order to be played fairly.
        b.   Group games usually involve a fantasy element.
        c.   Group games require strict division of roles and responsibilities.
        d.   Group games usually involve opposing teams.

14.   Group games permit children to shift roles. This contributes to the development of _____.
        (pp. 249-250)
        a.   out-group attitudes
        b.   perspective-taking skills
        c.   self-esteem
        d.   concrete operational thought

15.   Which of the following statements about friendship during the early school age period is most
       accurate? (pp. 250-251)
       a.   Children of this age rarely argue or quarrel during play.
       b.   Boys and girls usually play together.
       c.   Boys and girls tend to pick friends of the same sex.
       d.   Friendships are based on loyalty and trust.

16.   Which of the following is the best definition for the psychosocial concept of initiative?
       (p. 251)
       a.   sense of pride in a job well-done
       b.   active investigation of the environment
       c.   anxiety caused by having violated a cultural norm
       d.   a caring orientation toward relationships

17.   What is an adaptive outcome of experiencing guilt? (pp. 252-253)
       a.   curiosity and experimentation
       b.   a sense of remorse and attempts to set things right
       c.   intensive self-blame and feelings of worthlessness
       d.   there is no adaptive outcome related to experiences of guilt

18.   Which term refers to the psychological mechanism that signals when a violation of a forbidden
       behavior or thought is about to occur? (pp. 252-253)
       a.   fixation
       b.   guilt
       c.   phobia
       d.   mistrust

19.   Which of the following motives for parental identification is aroused by the following statement:
       "You and your father have the same sense of humor." (pp. 254-255)
       a.   perceived similarity
       b.   fear of loss of love
       c.   identification with the future
       d.   identification with the aggressor

20.   Which of the following has NOT been proposed as a motive for parental identification?
       (pp. 254-255)
       a.   need for status
       b.   identification with the aggressor
       c.   fear of loss of love
       d.   fear of failure

After completing the post-test, compare your score with your performance on the pre-test. Can you
identify areas where significant new learning has taken place? If you still have questions about some
sections of the chapter, read them again. Check the glossary. For additional test items, you may want to
go to the *Development Through Life* web site found by going to http://www.psychology.wadsworth.com.
If you still have questions, discuss them with your instructor.

Step Eight: Suggestions for Further Observation and Study

1. Find out what you can about gender-role standards among African American, Asian American, and Latino subcultures. In what ways do the ethnic groups differ in their expectations about the behavior role of male and female children?

2. Ask three children ages 4, 6, and 8 what it means to cheat and whether there are some reasons that cheating may be permissible. Compare their answers. Look for evidence of their understanding of the rules, their level of moral judgment, and their ability to take another person's perspective.

3. Talk with some parents about how their children coped with the process of attending kindergarten. How did this school transition affect the four developmental tasks for each child? What changes occurred in the groups influencing the child and in their relative importance in the child's life?

4. Interview children who are raised in alternative family structures (single parent, gay or lesbian parents, grandparents).Compare their reports of experiences with the limited research in this area from two-parent heterosexual households.

5. Watch an hour or two of children's television with a young early school age child. What are the themes of the programs you watched? What assumptions do television producers appear to make about the kinds of entertainment that are suitable for children? Know as the child to describe the television programs they just viewed. How do your interpretations vary?

6. Learning through Technology: InfoTrac®
    For further study, explore InfoTrac® College Edition, an online library. Go to
    http://www.infotrac-college.com and use the pass code that came on the card with your book. To learn more, look up the following search terms and subdivisions in InfoTrac®.

    GENDER IDENTITY
        Psychological Aspects
        Research
        Social Aspects

    MORAL DEVELOPMENT

    SELF-ESTEEM
        Analysis
        Psychological Aspects
        Research
        Social Aspects

    CHILDHOOD FRIENDSHIP
        Social Aspects
        Study and Teaching
        Surveys

    GUILT and/or SHAME

    KINDERGARTEN
        Curricula
        Research
        Social Aspects

    PRESCHOOL EDUCATION

    SCHOOL VIOLENCE
        History
        Personal Narratives
        Prevention
        Psychological Aspects
        Statistics
        United States

    GAY PARENTS and/or CHILDREN
        OF GAY PARENTS

CHAPTER NINE
Middle Childhood (6-12 Years)

Step One: Review the Chapter Outline

Developmental Tasks
    Friendship
    Concrete Operations
    Skill Learning
    Mathematics Ability
        Self-Evaluation
        Team Play
The Psychosocial Crisis: Industry versus Inferiority
    Industry
Case Study: Becca
    Inferiority
The Central Process: Education
The Prime Adaptive Ego Quality and the Core Pathology
    Competence
    Inertia
Applied Topic: Violence in the Lives of Children
    Consequences of Exposure to Violence
    Prevention Strategies
Chapter Summary

Step Two: Review the Chapter Objectives

- To clarify the role of friendship in helping children to learn to take the point of view of others, be sensitive to the norms and pressures of the peer group, experience closeness in relationships as well as to clarify negative consequences that result from social rejection and loneliness.
- To describe the development of concrete operational thought, including conservation, classification skills, combinatorial skills, and the child's ability to understand and monitor his or her own knowledge and understanding.
- To explore skill learning, including the presentation of a model for the process of acquisition of complex skills such as reading and the examination of societal factors that provide the context within which skill learning occurs.
- To analyze the development of self-evaluation skills, including self-efficacy, and ways that social expectations of parents, teachers, and peers contribute to a child's self-evaluation.
- To describe a new level of complexity in play as children become involved in team sports and athletic competition.
- To explain the psychosocial crisis of industry versus inferiority, the central process through which the crisis is resolved education, the prime adaptive ego quality of competence, and the core pathology of inertia.
- To explore the impact of exposure to violence on development during middle childhood.

Step Three: Take the Pre-Test

Answer these true/false questions before you read the chapter. The pages where material is discussed are indicated in the parentheses after each question. Use your performance as a guide to areas where you need to read carefully. The Answer Key for the pre-test can be found at the end of the study guide.

_____1. Around the world, millions of children in the age range of 6 to 12 are forced into slave labor. (p. 264)

_____2. Children who have secure attachments in infancy do not seek out friends and are usually unpopular during middle childhood. (p. 265)

_____3. Cognitive abilities such as perspective-taking are positively associated with friendship formation and social acceptance. (pp. 266-267)

_____4. Children who are mentioned as a best friend by several other children report that they are actually very lonely. (p. 267)

_____5. Same-sex best friend relationships at middle school age are often intimate in terms of self-disclosure and include feelings of love and closeness. (pp. 267-268)

_____6. Boys experience greater levels of caring and closeness with their best friends than do girls. (pp. 267-268)

_____7. Withdrawn children seem to lack the social skills that would allow them to gain acceptance by their age-mates. (p. 270)

_____8. Aggressive-withdrawn children are likely to have future adjustment problems and often require psychiatric treatment in adolescence and adulthood. (p. 270)

_____9. Schools don't have much influence on friendship formation during middle school age. (p. 259)

_____10. According to Piaget, children at about age 6 or 7 start to development formal operational reasoning. (pp. 268-270)

_____11. Children generally learn to conserve volume first, then mass, then weight. (p. 271)

_____12. Familiarity with the material plays a part in whether a child can conserve mass or number. (p. 271)

_____13. To perform a conservation task successfully, a child must understand how to group objects according to some dimension they share. (pp. 271-272)

_____14. It is possible to train children in the preoperational stage to solve conservation problems. (pp. 271-272)

_____15. By the age of 4 or 5, children can understand the way different sources of information contribute to their sense of knowing. (p. 275)

_____16. Metacognition is a child's ability to recognize the differences between feelings of certainty and uncertainty in their knowledge, and devise effective strategies for increasing their feelings of knowing. (p. 275)

_____17. Psychologists agree that there is only one true form of intelligence called *g*. (p. 275)

_____18. Complex skills are achieved by moving stepwise from the very simple components to the next more complex component. (pp. 275-276)

_____19. Reading is a skill that is largely determined by genetics. Family environment plays little if any role in the development of reading skills. (pp. 277-278)

_____20. American high school students express less stress and anxiety related to school than do Japanese and Chinese students. (pp. 278-279)

_____21. Children who have a low sense of self-efficacy tend to give up in the face of difficulty. (p. 280)

_____22. According to Bandura, four sources of information contribute to judgments of self-efficacy: enactive attainments, vicarious experience, verbal persuasion, and metacognition. (p. 280)

_____23. The psychosocial crisis of middle childhood is integrity versus inferiority. (p. 288)

_____24. Education is a way of passing on the wisdom and skills of a society to its young. (p. 291)

_____25. Competence is a belief in one's effectiveness. (p. 293)

Step Four: Read Chapter 9: Middle Childhood (6-12 Years)

Step Five: Review Basic Concepts By Matching Each Term and Its Definition

a. peers
b. classification
c. social expectations
d. industry
e. inferiority
f. self-efficacy
g. conservation
h. concrete operational thought
i. metacognition
j. education
k. division of labor

1. _____ A sense of pride and pleasure in acquiring culturally valued competencies.

2. _____ Views held by others about what would be appropriate behavior in a given situation or stage of development.

3. _____ Persons belonging to the same group, often on the basis of age or grade.

4. _____ A sense of confidence that one can perform the behaviors required in a given situation.

5. _____ Grouping objects according to some characteristics they have in common, including all objects that show the characteristic and none that do not.

6. _____ Thinking about and monitoring one's own thinking.

7. _____ A sense of incompetence and failure which is built on negative evaluations and lack of skill.

8. _____ The principle that complex tasks can best be performed when individuals assume special functions and coordinate their efforts.

9. _____ The concept that changes in shape or container do not alter the mass, weight, number, or volume of matter.

10. _____ The process of passing on the wisdom and skills of past generations to the young.

11. _____ In Piaget's theory, a stage of cognitive development in which rules of logic are applied to observable, physical relationships.

Step Six: Answer the Focusing Questions

1. How do friendships and peer interactions promote cognitive and social development during middle childhood? (p. 265-270)

2. Detail how the cognitive capacities for conservation, classification, and combinatorial processes influence a child's social relationships and self-evaluation? (pp. 270-275)

3. Describe how teachers' expectations influence a child's sense of industry or inferiority? (pp. 282-283)

4.   Does team play contribute to a child's cognitive development? If yes detail this relationship. (pp. 285-288)

5.   Create a program that details how parents and teachers can work together to promote a sense of industry and academic excellence in middle childhood age children. (pp. 288-293)

Step Seven: Take the Post-Test

1.   In which theory is middle childhood referred to as latency? (p. 264)
        a.   psychosocial theory
        b.   cognitive developmental theory
        c.   psychoanalytic theory
        d.   social learning theory

2.   Theories about development during middle childhood tend to emphasize _____. (p. 264)
        a.   sexuality
        b.   parent-child conflict
        c.   intellectual growth
        d.   emotional changes

3.   Peer interaction helps reduce _____. (pp. 266-67)
        a.   flexibility
        b.   egocentrism
        c.   assimilation
        d.   conservation

4.   One cognitive benefit of active involvement in the peer group is _____. (p. 267)
        a.   increased egocentrism
        b.   increased perspective-taking skills
        c.   increased emotional expressiveness
        d.   increased hopefulness

5.   Peer relations differ from parent-child relations in which of the following ways? (pp. 266-67)
        a.   peers never have conflicts about power, but parents and children do
        b.   peers are more equal in power than parents and children
        c.   peers have more power over one another than parents have over their children
        d.   peers have more resources than parents

6.   Which three concepts are central to the capacity to conserve? (pp. 271-272)
       a.   volume, space, relativity
       b.   operation, classification, reciprocity
       c.   identity, reversibility, reciprocity
       d.   classification, reversibility, ordering

7.   Classification skills require which ability? (pp. 273-274)
       a.   ordering subgroups in a hierarchy
       b.   conserving volume
       c.   manipulating numbers
       d.   taking another person's point of view

8.   Which statement about the development of complex behavioral skills is most accurate?
       (pp. 274-277)
       a.   Simple and complex components of skilled behavior are worked on at the same time.
       b.   Children must learn skills in a sequence from the simplest components to the more
              complex.
       c.   Skill learning is largely motor rather than perceptual, cognitive, or social.
       d.   Children of the middle-school-age years are likely to develop skills in only one or two
              areas.

9.   Which of the following statements about reading achievement is most accurate? (pp. 277-278)
       a.   Reading is a trial and error process that does not involve the use of strategies.
       b.   All children learn to read in the same manner.
       c.   One of the most important activities that promotes reading achievement is reading.
       d.   Parents have little influence on their child's reading achievement.

10.   Which of the following is a source of information upon which judgments of self-efficacy are
       based? (pp. 280-281)
       a.   grade in school
       b.   enactive attainments
       c.   fantasies
       d.   reversibility

11.   Children who doubt that they have the ability to succeed in a task are more likely to_____.
       (pp. 280-281)
       a.   give up
       b.   learn new skills
       c.   seek more difficult challenges
       d.   try harder

12.   Which of the following is likely to occur if a teacher has low expectations for a child's
       performance? (pp. 282-283)
       a.   The child will perform less well than if the teacher had higher expectations.
       b.   The child's performance will not be related to the teacher's expectations.
       c.   The child will do better to prove the teacher wrong.
       d.   The teacher will feel frustrated by the child's failure.

13. How do social expectations influence a child's self-evaluation? (pp. 281-284)
   a. social expectations influence a child's categorization skills
   b. social expectations create areas of talent
   c. social expectations foster out-group attitudes
   d. social expectations influence a child's confidence about success or failure

14. Which of the following is one of the three significant characteristics of team sports emphasized in the text? (pp. 285-286)
   a. friendship formation
   b. the principle of division of labor
   c. formation of group identity
   d. development of classification skills

15. Which of the following is an example of an in-group attitude fostered through experiences in team play? (pp. 287-288)
   a. One must always place personal goals ahead of team goals.
   b. Team victories can never overshadow personal failures.
   c. Team members are dependent on one another for success.
   d. Assisting the other team is unethical.

16. What is the psychosocial crisis of middle childhood? (p. 288)
   a. initiative versus guilt
   b. trust versus mistrust
   c. autonomy versus shame and doubt
   d. industry versus inferiority

17. Psychosocial theory states one's basic attitudes toward _____ are formed during the middle childhood period. (pp. 288-289)
   a. authority figures
   b. work
   c. children
   d. love

18. Cultures devise ways of passing on the wisdom and skills of past generations to its children through _____. (p. 291)
   a. self-efficacy
   b. education
   c. perspective taking
   d. division of labor

19. What does the term *contextualizing instruction* mean? (pp. 292-293)
   a. Grading the brightest children and teaching the lower ability children on a pass-fail basis.
   b. Creating a classroom environment that recognizes and builds upon children's prior experiences and previous knowledge.
   c. Creating a system of contracts in each subject.
   d. Insisting that all children adapt to the same school culture.

20.   A public health perspective on strategies to prevent violence focuses on _____. (pp. 297-298)
   a.   controlling aggressive children
   b.   a collaboration in identifying various layers of prevention
   c.   the criminal justice definitions and strategies for deterrence
   d.   first controlling the television programs geared toward children

After completing the post-test, compare your score with your performance on the pre-test. Can you identify areas where significant new learning has taken place? If you still have questions about some sections of the chapter, read them again. Check the glossary. For additional test items, you may want to go to the *Development Through Life* web site found by going to http://www.psychology.wadsworth.com. If you still have questions, discuss them with your instructor.

Step Eight: Suggestions for Further Observation and Study

1.   Visit an elementary school. What are the strategies used to promote a sense of industry? What kinds of student achievements seem to receive the most public recognition?

2.   Talk to parents and teachers of six to twelve year olds. Ask them the following questions: How do the social expectations of others, especially parents and teachers, influence one's own self-assessment and expectancies? What critical examples from their own experience can you identify in which your own assessment was substantially influenced, either positively or negatively, by what someone else thought you could accomplish?

3.   Think back on your own experiences as a member of a team. What did you learn about yourself, about other team members, and about the norms of your community? Did you have any coaches that were especially memorable? What did they do that was supportive of your personal development or that of other team members; what did they do that might have interfered with your personal development or that of other team members? If you were to advise young children, what would you tell them about becoming involved in competitive team experiences?

4.   Listen to the news media or look through recent popular press for articles about how communities are dealing with violence in the schools. What are the basic controversies that arise in attempting to reduce violence? How are schools and communities attempting to resolve these controversies? How well are the developmental needs of children taken into account as schools and communities devise strategies to reduce violence? Detail how this fits with your experiences of school violence in middle childhood.

5.   Learning through Technology: InfoTrac®
       For further study, explore InfoTrac® College Edition, an online library. Go to http://www.infotrac-college.com and use the pass code that came on the card with your book. To learn more, look up the following search terms and subdivisions in InfoTrac®.

BULLYING   SELF-EFFICACY
       Personal narratives
       Prevention
       Psychological Aspects
       Social Aspects   FAMILY VIOLENCE
                                                  Demographic Aspects
READING   Health Aspects
                                                  Psychological Aspects

VIOLENCE IN TELEVISION
Psychological Aspects

AGGRESSIVENESS IN CHILDREN

GAY PARENTS

INTELLECT and/or INTELLIGENCE
LEVELS

LEARNING DISORDERS
Care and Treatment
Diagnosis
Physiological Aspects
Psychological Aspects
Research
Social Aspects

COMMUNICATIVE DISORDERS

CHAPTER TEN
Early Adolescence (12-18 Years)

Step One: Review Chapter Outline

Developmental Tasks
    Physical Maturation
Case Study: Carly Patterson, Olympic Gymnast
    Formal Operations
    Emotional Development
    Membership in the Peer Group
    Romantic and Sexual Relationships
The Psychosocial Crisis: Group Identity Versus Alienation
    Group Identity
    Alienation
The Central Process: Peer Pressure
    Affiliating with a Peer Group
    Peer Pressure in Specific Areas
    Conflicts Between Belonging and Personal Autonomy
    Ethnic-Group Identity
The Prime Adaptive Ego Quality and the Core Pathology
    Fidelity to Others
    Dissociation
Applied Topic: Adolescent Alcohol and Drug Use
    Factors Associated with Alcohol Use
    Early Entry into Alcohol and Drug Use
Chapter Summary

Step Two: Review the Chapter Objectives

- To describe the patterns of physical maturation during puberty for females and males, including an analysis of the impact of early and late maturing on self-concept and social relationships.
- To introduce the basic features of formal operational thought, highlighting the new conceptual skills that emerge and factors that promote the development of formal operational thought.
- To examine patterns of emotional development in early adolescence, including three examples of emotional disorders: eating disorders, delinquency, and depression.
- To describe the further evolution of peer relations in early adolescence, especially the formation of cliques and crowds, and to contrast the impact of parents and peers during this stage.
- To characterize the development of sexuality with a special focus on the transition to coitus, the formation of a sexual orientation, and a detailed review of the factors associated with pregnancy and parenthood in adolescence.
- To describe the psychosocial crisis of group identity versus alienation; the central process through which the crisis is resolved, peer pressure, the prime adaptive ego quality of fidelity to others, and the core pathology of isolation.
- To review the patterns of adolescent alcohol and drug use and the factors associated with their use and abuse within a psychosocial framework.

Step Three: Take the Pre-Test

Answer these true/false questions before you read the chapter. The pages where material is discussed are indicated in the parentheses after each question. Use your performance as a guide to areas where you need to read carefully. The Answer Key for the pre-test can be found at the end of the study guide.

_____1.   During early adolescence, the chronological peer group is biologically far more diverse than it was during early or middle school age. (p. 303)

_____2.   Overall activity and amount of strenuous physical activity increase for girls in the age range 10-18. (p. 304)

_____3.   Generally boys are more dissatisfied with their physical appearance and body image during adolescence than girls are. (p. 307)

_____4.   For boys, growth during puberty does not take place at the same rate in all parts of the body. (pp. 307-308)

_____5.   In adolescence, cognitive functioning becomes more reflective, abstract and complex. (pp. 309-310)

_____6.   According to research findings about brain development, cerebral maturation is complete by age 7. (p. 310)

_____7.   One result of cognitive development that comes with formal operational thinking is the ability to think about changes that are likely to occur in the future. (pp. 310-311)

_____8.   Egocentrism may cause an adolescent to become preoccupied with their own thoughts. (p. 312)

_____9.   There are very few components of the typical high school curriculum that have the potential to stimulate formal operational reasoning. (pp. 313-314)

_____10.   Research has shown that adolescent boys and girls who are more physically mature also have more frequent thoughts and feelings about love. (pp. 315-316)

_____11.   Adolescent boys commit more delinquent crimes than girls, but the girls' crimes are more serious. (p. 317)

_____12.   Adolescent girls are more likely to experience depression than are adolescent boys. (p. 320)

_____13.   In most high schools, there is one leading crowd. The rest of the students hang out in small cliques that cannot be labeled or identified. (p. 321)

_____14.   From age 10 to 14, peers become more important than parents as sources of close emotional support. (p. 323)

_____15.   For white adolescent boys, the age of transition to sexual activity during adolescence is best predicted by the attitudes of family members, friends, and their own career aspirations. (pp. 325-327)

_____16.   For white adolescent girls, the strongest predictor of the age at transition to sexual activity is hormone levels. (pp. 325-327)

_____17.   People who have permissive views about sex are more likely to attend religious services and find more satisfaction in religious participation than those whose views about sex are not permissive. (pp. 325-327)

_____18.   The majority of U.S. teens report using a contraceptive at the time of their first intercourse. (p. 329)

_____19.   Infants born to mothers under age 17 are at greater risk for prematurity than those born to women in their 20s and 30s. (p. 330)

_____20.   In early adolescence, people form schema, integrated sets of ideas about the norms, expectations, and status hierarchies, of the salient groups in their social world. (p. 333)

_____21.   In resolving the psychosocial crisis of early adolescence, young people are only concerned with their membership in the peer group. (p. 336)

_____22.   Adolescence is the first time that children are aware of being a member of a group or claim an affiliation with a group. (p. 336)

_____23.   Adolescents may use alcohol in an attempt to increase the sense of physical arousal. (p. 341)

_____24.   Most adolescents believe that their parents disapprove of daily drinking or binge drinking. (pp. 341-342)

_____25.   Among 4th and 5th graders, being home alone frequently after school is associated with the likelihood of early alcohol use. (p. 343)

Step Four: Read Chapter 10: Early Adolescence (12-18 Years)

Step Five: Review Basic Concepts By Matching Each Term and Its Definition

a.	alienation		b.	anorexia nervosa
c.	egocentrism		d.	ethnic group identity
e.	formal operations		f.	group identity
g.	peer pressure		h.	sexual orientation
i.	secular growth trend		j.	depression
k.	clique		l.	crowd

1.   _____   A preference for same-sex, opposite-sex, or both sex targets of sexual interest and arousal.

2.   _____   A sense of isolation and separateness from others.

3. _____ A tendency observed since approximately 1900 for earlier attainment of adult height and sexual maturation.

4. _____ Expectations for conformity to group norms and sanctions for violation of norms.

5. _____ In Piaget's theory, the final stage of cognitive development characterized by abstract reasoning, hypothesis generating, and hypothesis testing.

6. _____ A disorder involving the inability to regulate eating behavior and a desire for extreme thinness.

7. _____ A large group of peers characterized by similar patterns of behavior, shared values, and interlocking friendship.

8. _____ A preoccupation with one's own logic, point of view, and way of understanding experience.

9. _____ A small friendship group of five to ten friends.

10. _____ The positive pole of the psychosocial crisis of early adolescence in which the person finds membership in a peer group.

11. _____ Feelings of sadness, loss of hope, and a sense of being overwhelmed by the demands of the world.

12. _____ Realizing that some of one's thoughts, feelings, and beliefs are influenced by membership in a specific racial, religious, or cultural group.

Step Six: Answer the Focusing Questions

1. List and describe the psychological changes that are generally triggered by the physiological changes of puberty. (pp. 303-309)

2. Detail how males and females respond differently to the physical changes of puberty. (pp. 304-308)

3.   List and describe the six new conceptual skills that are associated with the acquisition of formal operational thought. Give examples of life experiences that foster these types of formal operational thinking. (pp. 310-312)

4.   What are the basic characteristics of eating disorders, delinquency, and depression? What are some reasons these outcomes of emotional development are linked to adolescence? (pp. 315-321)

5.   How do parent-child relationships influence adolescent friendships? (pp. 323-324)

6.   Detail factors associated with initiation of sexual intercourse during adolescence. What are the most common problems and risks associated with adolescents' sexual behaviors? (pp. 324-327)

7.   Explain the four interconnected elements of group identity and provide examples of what kinds of experiences contribute to each of these elements. (pp. 334-335)

1.   The period of physical development when the reproductive system matures is called _____.
(p. 303)
    a.   menopause
    b.   puberty
    c.   plasticity
    d.   couvade

2.   Which pattern best characterizes the physical changes associated with puberty? (p. 305)
    a.   The height spurt occurs earlier for girls than for boys.
    b.   The height spurt occurs earlier for boys than for girls.
    c.   Menarche is the first sign of pubertal change for girls.
    d.   The presence of facial hair is the first sign of pubertal change for boys.

3.   Which of the following best describes physical maturation for adolescent males? (p. 307)
    a.   includes increased height, weight and muscle mass
    b.   occurs two years earlier than for females
    c.   is characterized by a uniform growth rate in all body parts
    d.   is usually accompanied by high levels of anxiety and dread

4.   One consequence of the secular trend is that children _____. (p. 308)
    a.   are more intelligent today than they were 100 years ago
    b.   are shorter than they were in the past
    c.   are more likely to be members of peer groups today than they were 100 years ago
    d.   reach adult height earlier today than they did 100 years ago

5.   In Piaget's theory of cognitive development, _____ is considered the final stage, which includes
an increase in abstract thinking and hypothesis testing. (pp. 310-311)
    a.   sensorimotor intelligence
    b.   preoperational thought
    c.   formal operational thought
    d.   concrete operational thought

6.   Which of the following is an example of egocentrism in early adolescence? (pp. 312-313)
    a.   Adolescents cannot separate actions from their effects.
    b.   Adolescents cannot separate their perspective from that of the listener.
    c.   Adolescents assume that others share their hypothetical construction of reality.
    d.   Adolescents are actively seeking stimulation and risk.

7.   Which of the following is a criticism of the concept of formal operational thought? (p. 315)
    a.   as children reach puberty, they all use formal reasoning
    b.   formal reasoning is not necessary for effective problem solving
    c.   formal reasoning is not a broad enough concept to encompass all the dimensions along
which cognitive functioning matures
    d.   in modern times, adolescents don't like learning methods that require rote memorization

8.	During adolescence, boys and girls show noticeably different levels of aggression and depression. Problems that result from directing aggression outward toward harming others are known as _____ problems. (p. 316)
a.	neurotic
b.	internalizing
c.	self-destructive
d.	externalizing

9.	Symptoms of worrying, moodiness, crying, difficulty sleeping, and loss of interest in daily activities are associated with _____. (p. 318)
a.	anorexia nervosa
b.	delinquency
c.	egocentrism
d.	depression

10.	Which of the following statements is most accurate? (pp. 317-318)
a.	For adolescents, carrying a gun is linked to starting fights and feeling that shooting people is justified in certain circumstances.
b.	Equal numbers of boys and girls carry guns to school.
c.	For adolescents, carrying a gun is no different from carrying a knife. They are both linked to a motivation for peer dominance and power.
d.	Carrying a weapon to school is very rare and observed only among extremely violent youth.

11.	Which of the following is offered as an explanation for why depression is more often observed among adolescent girls than boys? (pp. 320-321)
a.	depression is associated with fluctuations in estrogen
b.	adolescent girls have more problems than adolescent boys
c.	girls take the problems of their family and friends more to heart, leading to more emotional distress.
d.	depression associated with fluctuations in estrogen and girls taking problems of their family to heart

12.	What does it mean to say that adolescent peer groups have boundaries? (pp. 322-323)
a.	you can see the edge of the group when they walk along the halls of the school
b.	there are unspoken rules about who is included in the group
c.	academic goals and achievement levels differentiate the groups
d.	the groups differ in their access to money and other resources

13.	In the transition to coitus, which of the following factors is associated with having a less permissive attitude toward premarital sex and a greater willingness to delay sexual activity? (p. 327)
a.	early entry into puberty
b.	low academic aspirations
c.	strong religious values
d.	living in a step family

14. Which statement best describes the consequences of adolescent childbearing? (pp. 330-331)
    a.   teen childbearing increases the likelihood of living in poverty by age 27
    b.   teen childbearing increases the likelihood of getting early and consistent prenatal care
    c.   teen childbearing is associated with the birth of larger, healthier babies
    d.   teen mothers are more likely to finish high school than teens who get pregnant and have an abortion

15. A positive sense of _____ provides an early adolescent with confidence that he or she is meaningfully connected to society, has a cognitive map of the characteristics of the social landscape, and the skills to successfully engage in social life. (p. 333)
    a.   social referencing
    b.   group identity
    c.   social attachment
    d.   role enactment

16. What is the psychosocial crisis of early adolescence? (p. 333)
    a.   generativity versus stagnation
    b.   group identity versus alienation
    c.   individual identity versus identity confusion
    d.   hope versus diffidence

17. By resolving the psychosocial crisis of early adolescence in a positive direction, a young person gains confidence that he or she _____ (p. 333)
    a.   has achieved formal operational thought and can successfully use the related skills.
    b.   is able to graduate from high school and attend college.
    c.   can maintain egocentrism in the face of conflicting opinions.
    d.   is meaningfully connected to valued social groups.

18. What is one likely outcome of alienation during early adolescence? (pp. 335-336)
    a.   a keen sense of group belonging
    b.   the development of a sense of industry
    c.   uneasiness in the presence of peers
    d.   increased understanding about peer pressure

19. Why is a sense of ethnic group identity heightened in early adolescence? (pp. 339-340)
    a.   adolescents encounter new sanctions against cross-race friendships and dating
    b.   minority adolescents are highly valued within their peer group
    c.   there are few differences in values between parents and peers
    d.   the majority culture acknowledges the contributions of ethnic groups as part of its heritage

20. How do adolescents describe their parents' views about their alcohol use? Teens believe that _____ . (pp. 342-343)
    a.   parents accept their teens' drinking as a normal part of experimentation
    b.   parents definitely disapprove of teens that drink alcohol daily
    c.   parents consider teens' daily drinking as risky but acceptable
    d.   parents are generally unaware of their teens' use of alcohol

After completing the post-test, compare your score with your performance on the pre-test. Can you identify areas where significant new learning has taken place? If you still have questions about some sections of the chapter, read them again. Check the glossary. For additional test items, you may want to go to the *Development Through Life* web site found by going to http://www.psychology.wadsworth.com. If you still have questions, discuss them with your instructor.

Step Eight: Suggestions for Further Observation and Study

1. Make a list of the experiences in your own education that you believe have helped you to develop your formal operational reasoning skills.In which areas of intellectual functioning is your formal operational reasoning most fully developed? Why?

2. Think about your first date. Talk to friends, your parents, or other middle adults about their early dating experiences. What are some common positive and negative experiences associated with these first dates? In what ways have the cultural norms about dating changed from your parents' generation to your own? In what ways are early dating experiences opportunities for new learning about self and social relationships?

3. Why might adolescence be a time for heightened sensitivity around issues of ethnic identity? What are some examples of ways that members of an ethnic subculture might encounter conflicts with the predominant culture? What are some common strategies that adolescents use to cope with these conflicts?

4. Contact the director of an alcohol abuse prevention program or an alcohol abuse treatment program that focuses on youth. What are the primary components of these programs? How are the programs related to the psychosocial needs of early adolescents? How serious are problems associated with alcohol abuse among early adolescents in your community?

5. Find out more about athletically gifted and talented teens. Read a biography, visit some teen athletes' web sites, or visit the web site for the U.S. Junior Olympics to learn more about how young people are recruited, their training schedules, and how being a gifted teen athlete fits in with other aspects of adolescent development including schooling, family life, emotional development, and peer relations.

6. Find out more about suicide prevention, especially programs that focus on adolescents. Visit http://www.mentalhealth.org/suicideprevention.

7. Find out more about sex education programs and policies. Visit SIECUS, the Sexuality Information and Education Council of the United States at http://www.siecus.org.

8. Learning through Technology: InfoTrac®
For further study, explore InfoTrac® College Edition, an online library. Go to http://www.infotrac-college.com and use the pass code that came on the card with your book. To learn more, look up the following search terms and subdivisions in InfoTrac®.

PUBERTY
Secular Trend
Pubertal Timing

CONSTRUCTIVISM
Analysis
Research

EMOTIONAL DEVELOPMENT

EATING DISORDERS IN CHILDREN
Diagnosis
Prevention
Risk Factors

TEENAGE PREGNANCY
Causes
Prevention
Case Studies
Psychological Aspects

PEER PRESSURE IN
ADOLESCENCE
Analysis
Psychological Aspects
Social Aspects

GROUP IDENTITY
Ethnic Group

CHAPTER ELEVEN
Later Adolescence (18-24 Years)

Step One: Review the Chapter Outline

Developmental Tasks
    Autonomy from Parents
    Gender Identity
    Internalized Morality
    Career Choice
The Psychosocial Crisis: Individual Identity Versus Identity Confusion
    Individual Identity
    Identity Confusion
    Identity Formation for Males and Females
Case Study: Houston A. Baker, Jr.
The Central Process: Role Experimentation
    Psychosocial Moratorium
    Role Experimentation and Ethnic Identity
Case Study: Turning Points in the Identity Process
The Prime Adaptive Ego Quality and the Core Pathology
    Fidelity to Values and Ideologies
    Repudiation
Applied Topic: The Challenges of Social Life
    Unwanted Sexual Attention
    Binge Drinking
    Sexually Transmitted Diseases
Chapter Summary

Step Two: Review the Chapter Objectives

- To examine the concept of autonomy from parents and the conditions under which it is likely to be achieved.
- To trace the development of gender identity in later adolescence, including a discussion of how the components of gender role identification that were relevant during the early-school-age period are revised and expanded.
- To describe the maturation of morality in later adolescence with special focus on the role of new cognitive capacities that influence moral judgments and the various value orientations that underlie moral reasoning.
- To analyze the process of career choice, with attention to education and gender-role socialization as two major influential factors.
- To describe the psychosocial crisis of individual identity versus identity confusion; the central process through which this crisis is resolved, role experimentation; the prime adaptive ego quality of fidelity to values and ideals, and the core pathology of repudiation.
- To examine some of the challenges of social life in later adolescence that may result in high-risk behaviors.

Step Three: Take the Pre-Test

Answer these true/false questions before you read the chapter. The pages where material is discussed are indicated in the parentheses after each question. Use your performance as a guide to areas where you need to read carefully. The Answer Key for the pre-test can be found at the end of the study guide.

_____1.   Later adolescents who achieve autonomy come to discover and accept the similarities and differences between themselves and their parents through a process of alienation from their parents' love. (p. 348)

_____2.   Differentiation, emerges from family systems theory, and is the extent to which a social system, such as the family, encourages intimacy while supporting the expression of differences. (p. 349)

_____3.   One aspect of cognitive maturity that helps later adolescents be successful in living independently is the capacity to plan for the future. (p. 350)

_____4.   When parents are perceived as emotionally supportive and caring about their later adolescent's well-being, there is a risk that the adolescent will remain overly dependent and fail to achieve autonomy. (p. 350)

_____5.   Over 50% of men in the age range 20 to 24 live at home with one or more parents. (p. 350)

_____6.   Economic factors and social norms do NOT play a significant role in the timing of leaving home. It is actually more about personal choice. (pp. 350-351)

_____7.   About 80% of college freshmen say that an important reason for deciding to go to college was to get away from their parents' home. (pp. 350-351)

_____8.   After a period of role experimentation and introspection, late adolescents may choose to adopt the gender identity, morality, and career aspirations framework that was in place at the end of their high school years. (p. 353)

_____9.   The content of gender role standards differs for people at different stages of life. (p. 355)

_____10.   Later adolescents add a sexual dimension to their gender identity that did not play much of a role in their childhood gender-role identification. (pp. 355-356)

_____11.   Satisfaction with one's physical appearance provides an important basis for approaching social relations with a positive, optimistic outlook. (p. 358)

_____12.   Hormone levels are not a good predictor of sexual activity for females, but are for males. For females, social contexts are more predictive than hormones. (p. 356)

_____13.   Failure to disclose one's homosexuality and to continue to pass as heterosexual is typically associated with better mental health. (pp. 356-357)

_____14.   Exposure to a diversity of information, relationships, and world views stimulates moral reasoning. (pp. 358- 359)

_____15.   Longitudinal studies of moral development show that adults use levels of reasoning that are very similar to those of school-age children. (p. 359)

_____16.   A prosocial judgment is a moral judgment that involves a conflict between doing something helpful for someone else and meeting one's own needs. (p. 360)

_____17.   Continued education beyond high school is associated with career advancement and higher earnings. (p. 363)

_____18.   In the U.S. the median income for males who have a high school diploma is higher than that for females who have completed one to three years of college. (p. 363)

_____19.   Gender role socialization has no bearing on career decision-making. (p. 364)

_____20.   Most students who go to college are not very concerned about what kind of job they will find after they graduate. (p. 365)

_____21.   In Tiedeman's model of career decision making, the phases show a path from early career exploration to full integration in the profession. (pp. 366-368)

_____22.   In the contemporary U. S. labor market, companies appear to be replacing many part-time workers and consultants with a larger staff of permanent, white-collar professionals. (p. 368)

_____23.   Once the personal identity has been formed, the content and evaluation components remain stable over the life course. (pp. 369-370)

_____24.   A strong, secure parental attachment interferes with a person's ability to examine alternatives and establish an identity in later adolescence. (pp. 371-372)

_____25.   People who have experienced crisis and uncertainty and then make occupational and ideological commitments are considered to have a foreclosed identity. (p. 372)

Step Four: Read Chapter 11: Later Adolescence (18-24 Years)

Step Five: Review Basic Concepts By Matching Each Term and Its Definition

a.	prosocial moral judgments	b.	self sufficiency
c.	identity achievement	d.	identity foreclosure
e.	internalized morality	f.	negative identity
g.	psychosocial moratorium	h.	identity confusion
i.	role experimentation	j.	gender identity
k.	fidelity to values	l.	repudiation

1.   _____   Identity status in which, after crisis, a sense of commitment to family, work,

political, and religious values is established.

2. _____ A period of free experimentation before individual identity is achieved.

3. _____ The negative pole of the psychosocial crisis of later adolescence in which the person cannot make a commitment to any unified vision of the self.

4. _____ Making independent decisions, taking responsibilities for one's actions, and achieving some degree of financial independence.

5. _____ Identity status in which commitments are established without questioning or crisis.

6. _____ An integrated set of beliefs, attitudes, and values about oneself as a man or a woman in many areas of social life.

7. _____ The ability to commit to beliefs and goals despite some contradictions and ambiguities.

8. _____ Moral decisions involving a conflict between doing something helpful for someone else and doing something to meet one's own needs.

9. _____ A set of values, beliefs, and ethical principles that guide behavior.

10. _____ A clearly defined self-image that is contrary to the cultural values of the community.

11. _____ Rejection of the ideas, values, and groups that do not adhere to one's own beliefs.

12. _____ Participation in a variety of roles as a means of discovering one's role commitments.

Step Six: Answer the Focusing Questions

1. Detail how going to college influences the achievement of autonomy from parents. (pp. 350-351)

2. Describe how culture influences gender identity through its impact on gender-role standards, the expression of sexual impulses, and gender-role preferences. (pp. 353-358)

3.   List three challenges to Kohlberg's view of moral development. (pp. 359-361)

4.   Explain how gender socialization and career choice are related. (pp. 361-365)

5.   Describe phases of career-decision making. (pp. 366-368)

6.   Define each of the five identity statuses: achievement, foreclosure, moratorium, identity confusion, and negative identity. (pp. 371-373)

Step Seven: Take the Post-Test

1.   Which of the following best reflects autonomy from parents? (p. 349)
    a.   rejection of parents
    b.   going to college
    c.   children and parents accept one another's individuality
    d.   alienation from parents

2.   How is college choice related to wanting to be independent from parents? (pp. 350-351)
     a.   over 50% of college freshmen say they chose a college as far from home as possible
     b.   the majority of college freshmen say they chose a college that would allow them to live near home
     c.   reasons differ greatly in whether going to college reflects a desire for independence from parents
     d.   in order to show their independence, the majority of college freshmen go to school in a different state from where their parents live

3.   In what way do students who live on campus differ from those who live with their families during college? Students who live on campus _____ (p. 351)
     a.   have more positive thoughts about their parents as time goes along, whereas those who live at home have increasing conflict with parents.
     b.   become more distant from their parents than those who live on campus.
     c.   become more critical of their parents as they meet new friends and teachers with different ideas from those they learned at home.
     d.   contribute more to their family's living expenses than do those who live at home.

4.   Which of the following terms refers to a set of beliefs, attitudes, and values about oneself as a man or a woman in many areas of social life? (p. 353)
     a.   gender identity
     b.   androgyny
     c.   gender constancy
     d.   masculinity

5.   Which term refers to cultural expectations concerning the appropriate behavior for males and females? (p. 355)
     a.   gender constancy
     b.   identification
     c.   sex-role preference
     d.   sex-role standards

6.   Research on Kohlberg's theory of moral development finds that _____. (p. 359)
     a.   there is no stage-like progression in moral reasoning
     b.   conventional reasoning is the earliest form of moral reasoning
     c.   individuals cannot follow arguments about moral issues unless they are presented at exactly their own level of moral judgment
     d.   adults in many cultures use higher levels of moral reasoning than do children

7.   Which is characteristic of postconventional moral reasoning? (p. 359)
     a.   an awareness of the relativism of values
     b.   concern for maintaining the existing rule structure
     c.   concern about whether one's behaviors will be rewarded or punished
     d.   concern about whether one's behaviors will benefit one's friends and family members

8. When faced with a moral dilemma, some people are especially concerned about how to arrive at a solution that will result in the least harm for all concerned. Which of the following refers to this kind of moral orientation? (pp. 360-361)
    a. prohibitive moral orientation
    b. caring orientation
    c. justice orientation
    d. utilitarian orientation

9. Which of the following is a prosocial moral judgment? (p. 360)
    a. deciding to steal or let someone die
    b. deciding to lie or hurt someone's feelings
    c. deciding to forge a signature or let someone suffer
    d. deciding to give directions to someone who is lost even though it will make you late for an appointment

10. Which factor do high school and college students say plays the greatest role in their career decision-making? (p. 363)
    a. individual factors (talents, abilities)
    b. socioeconomic factors (social class, race)
    c. family factors (mother and father as role models)
    d. societal factors (education, mass media)

11. Which of the following is an example of how gender identity influences career choices? (p. 365)
    a. Men are more concerned about the status of their careers than women.
    b. Men are more concerned about interpersonal quality of instruction in their majors than women.
    c. Women base their career decisions on their parents' careers.
    d. Feminine women are most likely to seek employment in male dominated fields.

12. What is an advantage of delaying career choice until later adolescence or early adulthood? (p. 366)
    a. having a chance to select a marriage partner
    b. achieving greater self-insight
    c. more time for extracurricular activities in high school
    d. saving up enough money to start a business

13. Which of the following statements best characterizes Tiedeman's model of career decision-making? (pp. 348-350)
    a. Career decisions are based primarily on external rewards.
    b. Men make more logical decisions about careers than do women.
    c. Career decision making involves continuous interaction between the individual and the work context.
    d. The first phases of career decision making can be bypassed for those who have a college degree.

14. The two structural components of identity are _____ and _____. (p. 370)
    a. moratorium; mutuality
    b. content; evaluation
    c. congruence; androgyny
    d. positive; negative

15.   Which of the following marks the psychological close of later adolescence? (pp. 370-371)
        a.   getting married
        b.   learning to drive a car
        c.   having a child
        d.   forming a personal identity

16.   What criteria does James Marcia use to determine a person's identity status? (p. 372)
        a.   the experience of crisis or uncertainty
        b.   commitment to values and goals
        c.   alienation from the peer group
        d.   a combination of a and b

17.   Which of the statements about identity formation is true? (p. 374)
        a.   Identity achievement is associated with positive ego qualities for men but not for women.
        b.   Moratorium is a more anxiety-filled status for women than for men.
        c.   Vocational commitments are more central to the identity content for women than for men.
        d.   Men who have a foreclosed identity are flexible and optimistic.

18.   *Identity confusion* refers to which of the following? (pp. 373-374)
        a.   premature decisions about identity
        b.   commitment to values that are antagonistic to society
        c.   commitment to parental values
        d.   unintegrated roles and the absence of any commitment

19.   What is the central process for the resolution of the psychosocial crisis of individual identity versus identity confusion? (p. 375)
        a.   postconventional reasoning
        b.   turning points
        c.   role experimentation
        d.   negative identity

20.   In order for role experimentation to enhance the identity process, a young person needs to
        _____. (pp. 375-376)
        a.   avoid new experiences that might challenge their views
        b.   delay facing conflicting or contradictory information as long as possible
        c.   conform to the opinions and standards of valued adults
        d.   seek new information that can shed light on one's self concept

After completing the post-test, compare your score with your performance on the pre-test. Can you identify areas where significant new learning has taken place? If you still have questions about some sections of the chapter, read them again. Check the glossary. For additional test items, you may want to go to the *Development Through Life* web site found by going to http://www.psychology.wadsworth.com. If you still have questions, discuss them with your instructor.

Step Eight: Suggestions for Further Observation and Study

1.   Analyze the extent of your autonomy from your parents. In what areas are you still dependent on them? In what areas are you becoming self sufficient? What evidence do you have that they view you in a more autonomous light than they did during your early adolescence? Compare the relationship you have with your parents with the relationship they had with their parents at your age. How have historical and social trends changed the concept of autonomy from parents across one generation?

2.   What aspects of United States culture make it difficult to develop a clear sense of individual identity? Read Erik Erikson's *Identity: Youth and Crisis*, NY: W. W. Norton, 1968. How would you compare the emphasis he placed on the development of individual identity in the United States at that time with the focus on individual identity today?

3.   Investigate the availability of career-decision-making resources at your college or university. How are issues of gender identity, moral values, and family relationships addressed in career development materials? How do these aspects of your identity shape your career goals?

4.   In what ways does the college environment stimulate your work on identity formation? Examine each content area-vocational goals and values, interpersonal relations, political ideology, religious/moral values, values regarding family roles. In what ways do experiences in and out of class have an impact on your experience of crisis or commitment in each of these areas?

5.   Use the *Occupational Outlook Handbook* to learn more about job prospects and working conditions in fields that interest you. Visit www.bls.gov/oco/ to access information from the Bureau of Labor Statistics.

6.   Learning through Technology: InfoTrac®
      For further study, explore InfoTrac® College Edition, an online library. Go to http://www.infotrac-college.com and use the pass code that came on the card with your book. To learn more, look up the following search terms and subdivisions in InfoTrac®.

AUTONOMY FROM PARENTS

GENDER IDENTITY
    Psychological Aspects
    Social Aspects

SEXUAL ORIENTATION
    Psychological Aspects
    Personal Narratives
    Social Aspects

IDENTITY
    Identity Crisis
    Psychological Aspects
    Religious Aspects
    Social Aspects

SEXUAL HARASSMENT
    Cases
    Demographics
    Psychological Aspects
    Religious Aspects
    Social Aspects

CAREER CHOICE
    Surveys
    Planning
    Psychological Aspects
    Social Aspects
    Statistics

CHAPTER TWELVE
Early Adulthood (24-34 Years)

Step One: Review the Chapter Outline

Major Concepts in the Study of Adulthood
    Social Roles
    Life Course
    Fulfillment Theories
        Competence
        Self-Acceptance
        Self-Actualization
Developmental Tasks
    Exploring Intimate Relationships
        Readiness to Marry
        Selection of a Partner
        Case Study: How Love Makes its Way into a Relationship
        Cohabitation
        Partners of the Same Sex
        Adjustment During the Early Years of Marriage
        Adjustment in Dual-Earner Marriages
    Childbearing
        Fertility Rate
        Decisions about Childbearing
        The Dual Roles of Intimate Partner and Parent
        The Decision Not to Have Children
    Work
        Case Study: Jay Crowe
        The World of Work
        Poverty and Career Opportunities
        Career Phases and Individual Development
    Lifestyle
        Pace of Life
        Social Network
        Competing Role Demands
        Health and Fitness
The Psychosocial Crisis: Intimacy versus Isolation
    Intimacy
        Interaction Styles of Men and Women
        Intimacy in the Work Setting
    Isolation
        Loneliness
        Depression
        Fragile Identity
        Sexual Disorders
        Situational Factors
        Divergent Spheres of Interest
        Enmeshment
The Central Process: Mutuality Among Peers
The Prime Adaptive Ego Quality and Core Pathology

Step Two: Review the Chapter Objectives

- To identify and define selected concepts that are especially relevant for understanding development during adulthood, including social roles, life course, and fulfillment theories.
- To analyze the process of forming intimate relationships, including identifying and committing to a long-term relationship, the role of cohabitation in forming close relationships, and the challenges one faces in adjusting to the early years of marriage.
- To describe the factors associated with the decision to have children, the impact of childbearing on the intimate parental relationship, and the contribution of childbearing to growth in adulthood.
- To explore the concept of work as a stimulus for psychological development in early adulthood with special focus on the technical skills, authority relations, demands and hazards, and interpersonal relations in the work environment.
- To examine the concept of lifestyle as the expression of individual identity, with consideration for the pace of life, balancing competing role demands, building a supportive social network, and adopting practices to promote health and fitness.
- To define and describe the psychosocial crisis of intimacy versus isolation; the central process through which the crisis is resolved, mutuality among peers; the prime adaptive ego quality of love; and the core pathology of exclusivity.
- To analyze divorce as a life stressor in early adulthood, including factors contributing to it and the coping process.

Step Three: Take the Pre-Test

Answer these true/false questions before you read the chapter. The pages where material is discussed are indicated after each question. Use your performance as a guide to areas where you need to read especially carefully. The Answer Key for the pre-test can be found at the end of the study guide.

_____1.   The biological, psychological, and societal systems continue to interact in early adulthood. (p. 386)

_____2.   Social roles are reciprocal and require complementary role identification. (p. 387)

_____3.   An individual's social clock is the same as an individual's biological clock. (p. 388)

_____4. Fulfillment theory suggests a renewed interest in individual choice and growth in early adulthood. (pp. 389-390)

_____5. A factor associated with readiness to marry is achievement of some sense of identity. (p. 392)

_____6. Attending college tends to delay age at marriage, especially for women. (p. 393)

_____7. Men and women are similar in who they view as a desirable partner. (p. 395)

_____8. Marriages between partners who have cohabited are less likely to end in divorce than are marriages between partners who have not cohabited. (pp. 399-400)

_____9. Gay couples are more likely to break up; lesbian couples are more likely to stay together. (pp. 400-401)

_____10. The first years of marriage are filled with tension as couples struggle to adapt to each other. (p. 402)

_____11. In a study of communication in marriage, wives saw their husbands as more controlling than they would prefer. (pp. 402-403)

_____12. Negative communication, including hostile putdowns and nonverbal expressions, is more frequent among distressed than among happy couples. (pp. 402-404)

_____13. Dual earner couples are more resilient in the face of chronic stressors than single-earner couples. (p. 404)

_____14. Married men are more likely than married women to say that they would prefer to be childless. (pp. 405-406)

_____15. Recollections of one's childrearing environment are related to the level of marital satisfaction a person experiences after the birth of his/her first child. (pp. 407-408)

_____16. After a child is born, parents spend more time alone than they did before the baby was born. (pp. 407-408)

_____17. Women who have had four years or more of college are less likely to expect to be child free than women with less than four years of college. (p. 408)

_____18. Work has little influence over an individual's personal identity and achievement of intimacy. (p. 409)

_____19. The majority of people in the United States stay at their first job until they retire. (pp. 409-410)

_____20. The biggest challenge facing individuals in the transition from welfare to work is the lack of jobs that provide a living salary and benefits. (pp. 413-414)

_____21. The greatest concerns in the early career phase reflect the need to demonstrate competence and establish a satisfying lifestyle. (p. 414)

_____22. In the U.S. demands of the work setting often place women in conflict between expectations for commitment to work and commitment to motherhood. (pp. 415-416)

_____23. The work setting is not relevant for the establishment of intimacy between peers. (p. 419)

_____24. Contrary to many people's beliefs, research shows that men interact in a more intimate, open manner than women. (p. 419)

_____25. It is very unusual for a person who has been divorced to give any thoughts to or have any feelings for the former spouse once the divorce has been finalized. The legal end to the marriage ends the emotional attachment. (pp. 426-427)

Step Four: Read Chapter 12: Early Adulthood (24-34 Years)

Step Five: Review Basic Concepts By Matching Each Term and Its Definition

a.	social role	b.	life course
c.	social clock	d.	competence motivation
e.	dual-earner marriage	f.	intimacy
g.	isolation	h.	mutuality
i.	homogamy	j.	role strain
k.	lifestyle	l.	social integration

1. _____ A relatively permanent structure of activity, including the tempo of activity, the balance between work and leisure, and patterns of family and social relationships.

2. _____ Social expectations for changes in roles and responsibilities that are tied to age norms.

3. _____ Behaviors motivated by a desire for a new level of mastery.

4. _____ Married partners both of whom participate in the labor force.

5. _____ A crisis resolution in which a person remains psychologically distant from others.

6. _____ The ability to experience an open, supportive, tender relationship with another person, without the fear of losing one's identity.

7. _____ People are attracted to others who share important areas of similarity.

8. _____ The pattern of significant roles, events, and transitions a person experiences from infancy through later adulthood.

9. _____ The degree to which people are connected to others in the community especially through a shared value system.

10. _____ The ability of two people to meet each other's needs.

11. _____ A set of behaviors that have socially agreed-upon functions and an accepted code of norms.

12. _____ The conflict and competing demands made by several roles that the person holds simultaneously.

Step Six: Answer the Focusing Questions

1. Describe the life course and the two central themes of transitions and trajectories. (p. 388)

2. What are the three concepts from fulfillment theory that are relevant in the study of adulthood? (pp. 389-392)

3. What are the four phases of the mate selection process? What factors determine whether the relationship moves along or terminates? (pp. 374-379)

4. What are some of the adjustment issues in the early years of marriage? How does adjustment differ in dual-earner marriages? (pp. 402-405)

5.   What is the impact of the birth of a child on the marriage relationship? (pp. 405-408)

6.   How might the work setting stimulate new learning in early adulthood? (pp. 409-415)

7.   What are four factors that influence the formation of one's lifestyle in early adulthood? (pp. 415-417)

8.   What factors in the socialization of men and women pose barriers to the achievement of intimacy? (pp. 417-419)

9.   Discuss factors that account for divorce considering a national level, a community level, and couple level of analysis. (pp. 423-428)

Step Seven: Take the Post-Test

1.   Social roles are considered reciprocal and require _____. (pp. 387-388)
        a.   role loss
        b.   complimentary role identities
        c.   role gain
        d.   disengagement from a role

2.   The idea that there is an appropriate age for significant life events to occur is referred to as the
        _____. (p. 388)
        a.   life career
        b.   social clock
        c.   functional autonomy of motives
        d.   humanizing of values

3.   The term *life course* refers to _____. (p. 388)
        a.   the psychosocial crises an individual experiences from birth
        b.   the process of establishing an intimate relationship
        c.   Maslow's hierarchy of needs
        d.   integration and sequencing of work and family roles over time

4.   Which of the following are considered concepts associated with fulfillment theory? (pp. 389-390)
        a.   cohort, social role, social clock
        b.   competence, self-acceptance, self-actualization
        c.   transitions, trajectories
        d.   intimacy, isolation

5.   Wendell decided that he would no longer hide his emotions when involved in a relationship. His
        goal is to foster trust in a relationship by accepting himself. Which of the following concepts best
        describes his behavior? (p. 390)
        a.   competence motivation
        b.   role balance
        c.   self actualization
        d.   self acceptance

6.   The most important domain of life that contributes to a person's happiness and well-being is
        _____. (p. 392)
        a.   career advancement
        b.   having a satisfying marriage
        c.   raising children
        d.   living in one's own home

7.   Which of the following factors plays a part in moving a couple from phase III, deep attraction, to
        phase IV, "the right one" relationship? (pp. 394 and 397-398)
        a   potential loss of a confidante and companion
        b.   differences in interest
        c.   negative self-disclosure
        d.   physical attraction

8. During Phase II of the mate selection process, couples who continue to see each other often experience feelings of rapport and discover _____. (p. 394 and 397)
    a. basic similarities
    b. their own weaknesses
    c. mutual dislike of risk taking
    d. a "sense of the right one"

9. Happy couples are distinguished from distressed couples because they _____. (pp. 402-403)
    a. spend less time together
    b. are less likely to express their emotions
    c. can interrupt negative interactions before they become too unpleasant
    d. are more controlling in their interactions

10. High-quality, dual-earner marriages are more likely to be characterized by _____. (pp. 404-405)
    a. the presence of preschool-age children
    b. careers in traditional businesses such as law or accounting
    c. wives earning more than husbands
    d. an appreciation for one another's struggles and accomplishments

11. What impact does having children seem to have on the marital relationship in the first few years after the baby is born? (pp. 407-408)
    a. By the third year of marriage, parents have less marital satisfaction than non-parents.
    b. The percentage of leisure activities shared by husband and wife drops significantly for both parents and non-parents.
    c. During the third year of marriage, parents have a greater number of shared activities per day than non-parents, but very few when the child was not present.
    d. The number of shared activities per day increases for both parents and non-parents in the first three years of marriage.

12. The aspect of an individual's early career that deals with the decision-making structure, such as who evaluates one's work is called _____. (p. 412)
    a. authority relations
    b. technical skills
    c. hazards of the workplace
    d. the crystallization phase

13. One of the major sources of satisfaction in the workplace is the opportunity for _____. (pp. 412-413)
    a. supervision and evaluation
    b. exposure to intense emotions of clients
    c. friendship with co-workers
    d. competition with other workers

14. In the early career phase, what is considered the most common family concern? (p. 414)
    a. How can I establish a satisfying personal life?
    b. What is my role in the family as the children are grown?
    c. What is my role in the family after retirement from work?
    d. Should I begin a new career or spend more time with my family?

15. For most people, establishing a lifestyle requires balancing _____. (pp. 415-416)
    a. a series of psychosocial crises
    b. anxiety and depression
    c. a career ladder
    d. competing role demands

16. Which of the following is considered a characteristic of an intimate relationship? (pp. 417-418)
    a. One partner relies heavily on the judgment of the other and, therefore, does not have to make decisions.
    b. Each partner tries to outdo the other in expressions of independence.
    c. Partners experience mutual enrichment without losing their individual identities.
    d. Each person's identity is lost in order to create a blending of personalities.

17. If you move to a new town where you do not know many people, you are likely to experience _____ loneliness. (p. 420)
    a. chronic
    b. transcendental
    c. reflective
    d. situational

18. Kim and Lee realize that they can recognize each others' needs and are willing to modify their behavior in order to try to help the other one as needed. This is evidence of _____. (p. 422)
    a. mutuality between peers
    b. isolation
    c. social integration
    d. a mentoring relationship

19. What is the relationship between family history of divorce and the likelihood of divorcing as an adult? (p. 426)
    a. There is no relationship between experiencing parents' divorce as a child and divorcing as an adult.
    b. Individuals who experience parental divorce as children are less likely to divorce as adults.
    c. Individuals who experience parental divorce as children are more likely to divorce as adults.
    d. Women who experience their parents' divorce as children are more likely to divorce as adults: this is not true for men.

20. Which of the following statements about coping with divorce is true? (p. 427)
    a. Divorced people are likely to retain an attachment to their former spouse which interferes with adjustment.
    b. Divorced people are no different from those people who are married and never divorced with respect to life satisfaction.
    c. Divorced people cope more effectively when they isolate themselves from family and friends.
    d. All of these are true.

After completing the post-test, compare your score with your performance on the pre-test. Can you identify areas where significant new learning has taken place? If you still have questions about some sections of the chapter, read them again. Check the glossary. For additional test items, you may want to go to the *Development Through Life* web site found at http://www.psychology.wadsworth.com. If you still have questions, discuss them with your instructor.

Step Eight: Suggestions for Further Observation and Study

1.   Map your life course. Include details about events that have influenced the direction of your occupational and family careers. Make projections about important transitions in the future.

2.   Trace the history of your most recent intimate relationship. What factors were associated with the initial attraction? How far did the relationship progress (i.e., Phase II, III, IV)? What factors were involved in moving the relationship to the next phase or in terminating the relationship? In general, how useful is this model for understanding the history of a real-life example?

3.   Visit with an attorney or a judge who deals with divorce. Then visit with a marriage and family therapist who works with couples going through divorce. Contrast their views. What are the primary reasons for divorce? What steps do they think couples could take to prevent divorce? What resources are available in your community to assist couples who are experiencing serious marital conflict?

4.   Learning through Technology: InfoTrac®
        For further study, explore InfoTrac® College Edition, an online library. Go to http://www.infotrac-college.com and use the pass code that came on the card with your book. To learn more, look up the following search terms and subdivisions in InfoTrac®.

ADULTHOOD
- Life Course
- Competence
- Self Acceptance
- Self Actualization
- Social Role

INTIMATE RELATIONSHIPS
- Cohabitation
- Dual Earner Marriages
- Intimacy
- Love
- Marriage
- Sexuality

PARENTHOOD
- Childlessness
- Pregnancy

CAREER DEVELOPMENT

HEALTH AND FITNESS

SINGLEHOOD

DIVORCE
- Child Custody
- Marital Conflict
- Non-custodial Parents
- Single Parents

DEPRESSION

CHAPTER THIRTEEN
Middle Adulthood (34-60 Years)

Step One: Review the Chapter Outline

Developmental Tasks
    Managing a Career
        Achieving New Levels of Competence in the World of Work
        Midlife Career Changes
        Balancing Work and Family Life
        The Impact of Joblessness
    Nurturing an Intimate Relationship
        A Commitment to Growth
        Case Study: The Struggle for Commitment to Growth in a Vital Marriage
        Effective Communication
        Creative Use of Conflict
        Preserving Passion in Long-Term Relationships
    Expanding Caring Relationships
        Parenting
        Caring for One's Aging Parents
        Case Study: A Daughter Cares for her Ailing Mother
    Managing the Household
        Managing Resources and Meeting Needs
        Building Networks and Coalitions
        Remarriage and Blended Families
        One-Parent Families
        People Who Live Alone
The Psychosocial Crisis: Generativity Versus Stagnation
        Generativity
            Measuring Generativity
        Case Study: My Leadership Journey
        Stagnation
The Central Process: Person-Environment Interaction and Creativity
        Person-Environment Interaction
        Creativity
The Prime Adaptive Ego Quality and the Core Pathology
        Care
        Rejectivity
Applied Topic: Discrimination in the Workplace
        Disparities in Income and the Occupational Structure
       How Discrimination Perpetuates Itself
       Psychosocial Analysis: Discrimination and Coping
Chapter Summary

Step Two: Review the Chapter Objectives

- To examine the world of work as a context for development, focusing on interpersonal demands, authority relations, and demands for the acquisition of new skills; considering midlife career changes; examining the interaction of work and family life; and examining the impact of joblessness in middle adulthood.
- To examine the process of maintaining a vital intimate relationship in middle adulthood, especially a commitment to growth, effective communication, creative use of conflict, and preserving passion.
- To describe the expansion of caring in middle adulthood as it applies to two specific roles: that of parent and that of an adult child caring for one's aging parents.
- To analyze the tasks required for effective management of the household and their impact on cognitive, social, and emotional development of family members.
- To explain the psychosocial crisis of generativity versus stagnation and the central processes through which the crisis is resolved: person-environment interaction and creativity. To define the primary adaptive ego strength of care and the core pathology of rejectivity.
- To apply a psychosocial analysis to the issue of discrimination in the workplace, with special focus on the cost to society as well as to the individual when discrimination operates to restrict career access and advancement.

Step Three: Take the Pre-Test

Answer these true/false questions before you read the chapter. The pages where material is discussed are indicated after each question. Use your performance as a guide to areas where you need to read especially carefully. The Answer Key for the pre-test can be found at the end of the study guide.

_____1.   A person can only be viewed as having an occupational career if his or her work roles follow an orderly, progressive pattern in related fields. (pp. 432-433)

_____2.   Achieving new levels of competence is an aspect of managing a career. (p. 433)

_____3.   New competitive pressures on corporations and business organizations are leading to greater demands for specialization. (p. 435)

_____4.   The interpersonal values of leaders in a work group influence the work environment. (p. 434)

_____5.   Midlife career changes are always viewed as positive life changes, bringing new and more meaningful opportunities. (p. 436)

_____6.   The idea of spillover is illustrated when feelings of success at work contribute to marital satisfaction. (p. 437)

_____7.   In families where both husband and wife are employed, most couples expect to share responsibility for child care and household tasks equally. (pp. 437-439)

_____8.	Even if employed, the threat of a job loss can impact an individual's psychosocial development in middle adulthood. (p. 440)

_____9.	Marriage during the middle adulthood years is more likely to be considered a vital relationship if the couple agrees not to argue. (p. 442)

_____10.	Couples who are happy are more likely to have frequent interactions with each other. (p. 442)

_____11.	Constructive use of conflict is viewed as an important component in order to maintain a vital marriage relationship. (pp. 442-443)

_____12.	For those who are sexually active, there are no changes in sexual responsiveness that occur during middle adulthood. (pp. 444-445)

_____13.	A child's developmental level has no impact on a parent's individual development. (p. 446)

_____14.	When adult children leave home, their parents typically become depressed and withdrawn. (p. 448)

_____15.	Since the 1970's, the number of middle adults whose parents are living has gradually declined. (pp. 448-449)

_____16.	In general, adult children have a greater sense of obligation for their aging parents than their parents expect them to have. (pp. 449-450)

_____17.	Because sons tend to earn more than daughters, sons assume much more of the responsibility for the caregiving of their aging parents than daughters. (p. 450)

_____18.	Cultural norms for independence and self-sufficiency make it difficult for aging parents to accept help from their children. (p. 451)

_____19.	The fastest growing segment of people who become homeless is single, unemployed adult men. (p. 456)

_____20.	According to the text, the developmental task of household management draws upon and stimulates leadership skills. (p. 452)

_____21.	Generativity is critical to the survival of any society. (p. 457)

_____22.	There is no way to measure generativity because it is very abstract. (pp. 458-459)

_____23.	The social environment, including family, work setting, and neighborhood are integral to the central process for resolving the crisis of generativity versus stagnation. (pp. 460-461)

_____24.	A creative response redefines the situation and opens the way to new possibilities. (pp. 461-462)

_____25.   Discrimination in the work place helps promote societal generativity. (p. 464)

Step Four: Read Chapter 13: Middle Adulthood (34-60 Years)

Step Five: Review Basic Concepts By Matching Each Term and Its Definition

a. generativity   b. stagnation
c. discrimination   d. creativity
e. parenting alliance   f. managerial resourcefulness
g. person-environment interaction   h. vital marriage
i. filial obligation   j. care
k. rejectivity   l. role overload

1. _____   The willingness to abandon old forms or patterns and to think in new ways.

2. _____   A relationship in which there is strong commitment to an enduring marital dyad, and in which each person experiences increasing fulfillment and satisfaction.

3. _____   The capacity of a spouse to acknowledge, respect, and value the parenting roles and tasks of the partner.

4. _____   A child's sense of responsibility for the care and support of his/her parents.

5. _____   A process of reciprocal influence between individual needs, talents, and resources, and the opportunities and demands of social and physical settings.

6. _____   Decisions about a person, based on that person's membership in a group rather than on the person's competence and merit.

7. _____   Multiple roles lead to too many demands and expectations to handle in the allotted time.

8. _____   A lack of psychological movement or growth which results from self-aggrandizement or from the inability to cope with developmental tasks.

9. _____   A capacity to nurture and sustain other people, ideas or products.

10. _____   The desire to improve the quality of life for future generations.

11. _____   An unwillingness to embrace certain groups or ideas, and to see them as targets of justified hostility.

12. _____   Flexible, creative problem solving in the workplace, particularly when facing new problems and changing conditions.

Step Six: Answer the Focusing Questions

1.   What are the major challenges in managing a career in middle adulthood? How might economic or historical factors impact career management in middle adulthood? (pp. 432-442)

2.   Define the concept of a vital marriage. Explain how the following characteristics contribute to a long-lasting, happy marriage: characteristics of the partners as individuals; the partners' interpersonal interactions; and the partners' commitment to nurturing the future of the relationship. (pp. 442-446)

3.   Expanding caring relationships is a developmental task of middle adulthood. Compare and contrast how parenting and caring for an aging parent contribute to adult development. What are some examples of new learning that may emerge in these two roles? (pp. 446-451)

4.   Creativity is a process associated with generativity. For each of the following household management tasks, provide an example of creative problem solving and relate how each task helps an individual achieve generativity. (pp. 461-463)

Managing financial resources:

Keeping the house clean and safe:

Maintaining relationships with friends and family:

5.	Link the experience of homelessness to the psychosocial crisis of generativity versus stagnation, the prime adaptive ego quality of care, and the core pathology of rejectivity. (p. 456)

6.	List and explain the factors that account for race, ethnic, and gender discrimination in the workplace. (pp. 463-466)

Step Seven: Take the Post-Test

1.	During middle adulthood, which of the following changes is expected to occur? (p. 432)
	a.	greater concern for the well-being of future generations
	b.	decreased emphasis on intellectual attainment
	c.	greater concern about peer approval
	d.	less openness about oneself

2.	Which statement best describes the relationship between work and an individual in middle adulthood? (p. 433)
	a.	Work plays a minor role in terms of psychosocial development.
	b.	There is reciprocity between work and individual development.
	c.	No relationship exists between work and individual development.
	d.	Psychosocial development influences work, but work does not influence psychosocial development.

3.	Career advancement in middle adulthood requires an individual to assume new levels of _____. (p. 434)
	a.	subordination
	b.	discrimination in occupational structure
	c.	exposure to physical and mental hazards
	d.	leadership

4.	Which of the following is NOT included in the text as a reason for an individual to experience a midlife career change? (pp. 436-437)
	a.	The first career no longer meets one's life goals.
	b.	The first career ends due to physical decline.
	c.	The first career reaches an early peak and no longer offers opportunities for advancement.
	d.	The first career resulted in so much success, the person decides to retire.

5. Link the experience of homelessness to the psychosocial crisis of generativity versus stagnation, the prime adaptive ego quality of care, and the core pathology of rejectivity. (p. 456)

6. List and explain the factors that account for race, ethnic, and gender discrimination in the workplace. (pp. 463-466)

Step Seven: Take the Post-Test

1. During middle adulthood, which of the following changes is expected to occur? (p. 432)
    a. greater concern for the well-being of future generations
    b. decreased emphasis on intellectual attainment
    c. greater concern about peer approval
    d. less openness about oneself

2. Which statement best describes the relationship between work and an individual in middle adulthood? (p. 433)
    a. Work plays a minor role in terms of psychosocial development.
    b. There is reciprocity between work and individual development.
    c. No relationship exists between work and individual development.
    d. Psychosocial development influences work, but work does not influence psychosocial development.

3. Career advancement in middle adulthood requires an individual to assume new levels of _____. (p. 434)
    a. subordination
    b. discrimination in occupational structure
    c. exposure to physical and mental hazards
    d. leadership

4. Which of the following is NOT included in the text as a reason for an individual to experience a midlife career change? (pp. 436-437)
    a. The first career no longer meets one's life goals.
    b. The first career ends due to physical decline.
    c. The first career reaches an early peak and no longer offers opportunities for advancement.
    d. The first career resulted in so much success, the person decides to retire.

5.	Which term refers to the need to handle too many demands from work and family life in the time available? (p. 437)
	a.	role ambiguity
	b.	role overload
	c.	role confusion
	d.	role enactment

6.	Which of the following is a characteristic of a vital marriage? (p. 443)
	a.	couple is committed to individual and couple growth
	b.	communication not needed because so much is already understood
	c.	conflict is avoided
	d.	levels of complaining and negative communication increase

7.	Which of the following is a characteristic of harmonious, long-lasting marriages? (p. 442)
	a.	a high level of complaints
	b.	little time together, thus little chance to disagree
	c.	the partners are even-tempered and warm-hearted
	d.	absence of conflict

8.	Which of the following statements best describes the contributions of parenting to adult development? (pp. 446-449)
	a.	Because of the tedium and repetition of parenting, it makes very little contribution to an adult's development.
	b.	Parenthood brings new demands for flexibility, creative problem solving, and value clarification.
	c.	Parenting has a significant impact on adult development only after the children have left the home.
	d.	Parenthood creates role overload and therefore prevents adult development.

9.	Which of the following statements best describes how parenting may promote adult development? (pp. 446-449)
	a.	Children have no influence on a parent's development.
	b.	Parents often regress to the developmental level of their children.
	c.	Parenting allows adults to remain in control and to exercise authority, thereby sustaining their sense of power.
	d.	Parenting provides a complex and changing context for problem solving and the enactment of personal values.

10.	Which of the following terms refers to the ability of a spouse or partner to convey respect and value for the parenting tasks and roles of his or her partner? (p. 446)
	a.	Parenting alliance
	b.	Authoritative parenting
	c.	Passive parenting
	d.	Parental monitoring

11.   The term *filial obligation* refers to _____. (p. 450)
      a.   finding creative solutions to daily problems
      b.   a child's sense of responsibility to his/her parents
      c.   perceived duty by a parent to care for one's children
      d.   an ability to understand a child's developmental levels

12.   Ann and Harold are in their late 70s. They are beginning to have problems performing some basic household tasks. According to research findings, from whom are they most comfortable receiving help? (p. 451)
      a.   their neighbors
      b.   a social service agency
      c.   their adult children
      d.   members of their church

13.   Managing a household is a developmental task of middle adulthood that requires _____. (pp. 452-454)
      a.   leadership skills
      b.   problem solving
      c.   financial management
      d.   all of the above

14.   Which of the following is considered a contributing factor to the increased number of families with children who are homeless? (p. 457)
      a.   decline in the purchasing power of the minimum wage
      b.   increased kinship support
      c.   the clustering of low-income housing in urban areas
      d.   the large number of women with children who are living in rural areas

15.   Which of the following best describes *generativity*? (p. 457)
      a.   an ability to self disclose in an intimate relationship
      b.   a commitment to improving societal conditions for future generations
      c.   an integration of past core pathologies with current goals
      d.   a commitment to skill development and career advancement

16.   If an individual has a sense of generative concern, then he/she typically _____. (pp. 458-459)
      a.   has narcissistic tendencies
      b.   is not able to fulfill role obligations
      c.   is self-absorbed with career goals
      d.   wants to make a difference in the lives of others

17.   Which of the following is associated with a sense of stagnation? (p. 460)
      a.   people who live alone
      b.   single parents
      c.   people who are self-absorbed
      d.   none of the above

18. In middle adulthood, resolution of the psychosocial crisis often requires novel solutions. This implies a need for _____. (pp. 461-462)
    a. conformity
    b. post conventional morality
    c. spillover
    d. creativity

19. How does status influence person environment interaction? (pp. 460-461)
    a. People with lower status have more alternatives to change or modify their environments.
    b. People with lower status have more opportunities to have their achievements acknowledged and valued.
    c. People with higher status have greater access to environmental resources and more power to modify the environment.
    d. People with higher status have less need for environmental supports.

20. Rejectivity may become _____. (pp. 463-464)
    a. a basis for discrimination in the workplace
    b. a form of creative problem solving
    c. a way of meeting one's parents' needs for filial obligation
    d. an individual's ego strength in later adulthood

After completing the post-test, compare your score with your performance on the pre-test. Can you identify areas where significant new learning has taken place? If you still have questions about sections of the chapter, read them again. Check the glossary. For additional test items, you may want to go to the *Development Through Life* website found at http://www.psychology.wadsworth.com. If you still have questions, discuss them with your instructor.

Step Eight: Suggestions for Further Observation and Study

1. Talk to your parents about their perceptions of middle adulthood. What challenges have they faced in trying to balance work and family life? What have been their major sources of satisfaction?

2. Look further into international and cross-national research on work/family facilitation. To what extent do the challenges facing U.S. workers confront people in other countries? What workplace policies exist in other countries that help support work/family facilitation?

3. Families are unique and are associated with many lifestyles. In this and previous chapters, various family structures and lifestyles have been examined, such as the single lifestyle, dual-career couples, childless couples, single-parent families, gay and lesbian parents, blended families, and families with various cultural value systems. Select one or two of these family lifestyles. Identify some of the difficulties and benefits individuals in these families may have in balancing work and family roles.

CHAPTER FOURTEEN
Later Adulthood (60-75 Years)

Step One: Review the Chapter Outline

Developmental Tasks
    Accepting One's Life
    Promoting Intellectual Vigor
        Connecting Theory and Research to Life: Age and Workplace Productivity
Redirecting Energy to New Roles and Activities
        Human Development and Diversity: Intergenerational Relationships in Various Ethnic Groups
        Technology and Human Development: The Use of the Internet among Older Adults
Developing a Point of View about Death
    Case Study: Morrie Schwartz Reflects on his Views about Death
The Psychosocial Crisis: Integrity versus Despair
    Integrity
    Despair
The Central Process: Introspection
The Prime Adaptive Ego Quality and the Core Pathology
    Wisdom
    Disdain
Applied Topic: Retirement
    Adjustment to Retirement
        Case Study: Retirement as a Release From Tedious Work
    The Future of Retirement
Chapter Summary

Step Two: Review the Chapter Objectives

- To explore the construct of life satisfaction in later adulthood and factors associated with subjective well-being.
- To describe factors that promote intellectual vigor with a focus on memory, postformal operational thought, crystallized and fluid intelligence; and to consider the interaction of heredity and environment on intelligence in later life.
- To examine the process of redirecting energy to new roles and activities with special focus on role gain, such as grandparenthood; role loss, such as widowhood; and new opportunities for leisure.
- To describe the development of a point of view about death.
- To explain the psychosocial crisis of integrity versus despair, the central process of introspection, the prime adaptive ego quality of wisdom, and the core pathology of disdain.
- To apply theory and research to understanding the process of adjustment to retirement in later adulthood.

Step Three: Take the Pre-Test

Answer these true/false questions before you read the chapter. The pages where material is discussed are indicated in the parentheses after each question. Use your performance as a guide to areas where you need to read carefully. The Answer Key for the pre-test can be found at the end of the study guide.

_____ 1.	Psychosocial theory assumes that there are new opportunities for growth in later adulthood. (p. 470)

_____ 2.	The integrating theme of later adulthood is the preservation of one's memory. (p. 470)

_____ 3.	Accepting one's life is considered a developmental task of later adulthood. (p. 471)

_____ 4.	A personality dimension described as *extroversion* is consistently associated with measures of well being, happiness, and security. (p. 473)

_____ 5.	Optimism is a personality characteristic that is linked to well-being in later adulthood. (p. 474)

_____ 6.	Physical health is unrelated to experiencing a sense of life satisfaction and acceptance. (p. 474)

_____ 7.	Cognitive functioning in later adulthood is considered stable and unidimensional. (p. 475)

_____ 8.	Age is directly associated with declines in short-term memory. (p. 476)

_____ 9.	Long-term memory is often referred to as a storehouse of a lifetime of information. (p. 476)

_____ 10.	Fluid intelligence is the ability to impose organization on information and to generate new hypotheses. (p. 478)

_____ 11.	An appropriate construct to understand the interaction of heredity and environment on intelligence in adulthood is reaction range. (p. 479)

_____ 12.	Grandparents tend to contribute to anxiety in their grandchild's life especially during times of stress. (pp. 481-482)

_____ 13.	In the United States, intergenerational family relationships are very unusual. (pp. 481-482)

_____ 14.	Most older widowers tend to remarry, while the majority of widows tend to live alone. (p. 486)

_____ 15.	Widows suffer greater increases in depression following the loss of their spouse than do widowers. (pp. 486-487)

_____ 16.	The development of a perspective on death is continuous and begins in childhood. (p.490)

_____ 17.	Researchers have found that individuals follow a single, typical path in the dying process. (p. 490)

_____ 18.	The psychosocial crisis of later adulthood is integrity versus disdain. (p. 493)

_____ 19.	In psychosocial theory, integrity refers to the ability to accept the facts of one's life and to face death without great fear. (p. 493)

_____ 20. Ageism contributes to some older adults' feeling of despair. (p. 493)

_____ 21. Through reminiscence a person can bring meaning to past life experiences and become more fearful regarding death and dying. (p. 494)

_____ 22. Memory, problem-solving abilities, and information processing all influence an adult's capacity to introspect which is the central process of later adulthood. (pp. 494-495)

_____ 23. In later life, most people expect to achieve the prime adaptive ego quality of wisdom. (p. 495-496)

_____ 24. The concept of disdain conveys a meaning of flexibility and openness to different ideas and is a result of introspection in later life. (p. 496)

_____ 25. Retirement is a very old concept. For the past 100 years at least, the majority of working men expected to retire at age 65. (pp. 496-497)

Step Four: Read Chapter 14: Later Adulthood (60-75 Years)

Step Five: Review Basic Concepts By Matching Each Term and Its Definition

a.	integrity		b.	despair
c.	wisdom		d.	disdain
e.	hospice		f.	retirement
g.	crystallized intelligence		h.	fluid intelligence
i.	introspection		j.	reminiscence
k.	bereavement		l.	the SOC model

1. _____ The emotional suffering following the death of a loved one.

2. _____ A feeling of scorn for the weakness of oneself and others.

3. _____ The ability to bring knowledge gained through past experience into play in appropriate situations.

4. _____ Deliberate self-evaluation and review of thoughts and feelings.

5. _____ The psychological state of withdrawal from one's work and a new orientation towards work.

6. _____ An integrated system of medical, nursing, counseling, and spiritual care for the dying person and his/her family.

7. _____ The ability to accept the facts of one's life and face death without great fear.

8. _____ The ability to impose organization on information and to generate new hypotheses.

9. _____ A way of explaining the process of coping with aging that emphasizes identifying priorities and allocating resources to these priorities in order to preserve an optimal level of functioning.

10. _____ Feeling of loss of all hope and confidence.

11. _____ A type of expert knowledge that reflects sound judgment and good advice in the face of typically high levels of uncertainty.

12. _____ The process of thinking or telling about past experiences.

Step Six: Answer the Focusing Questions

1. What are the four major developmental tasks associated with later adulthood? How are they related to the ability to resolve the psychosocial crisis of integrity versus despair? (pp. 471-493)

2. List four problems that make it difficult to study intelligence in later life. (pp. 475-476)

3. What are some suggestions you would give to an older adult for promoting optimal intellectual functioning? (pp. 475-479)

4. In what ways do grandparenthood and widowhood allow for the redirection of energy to new roles in later adulthood? (pp. 481-485

5.   What are the primary benefits of leisure activities for older adults? How typical is it for older adults to be involved in various types of leisure activities? (pp. 487-490)

6.   What are some of the challenges of coping with death that are especially challenging for those in later adulthood? (pp. 490-493)

7.   How does the process of introspection help older adults resolve the psychosocial crisis of integrity versus despair? (pp. 494-495)

8.   What are the basic features of wisdom? What kinds of life experiences promote the development of wisdom? (pp. 495-496)

9.   Describe some challenges individuals face in trying to adjust to retirement. How is the ability to cope effectively with retirement related to the developmental tasks of later adulthood? (pp. 496-498)

Step Seven: Take the Post-Test

1.   The integrating theme of life in later adulthood is _____. (p. 470)
a.   a search for personal meaning
b.   a sense of industry
c.   a search for identity
d.   a longing for intimacy

2.   Which of the following is NOT a developmental task of later adulthood? (p. 471)
a.   acceptance of one's life
b.   developing a point of view about death
c.   redirecting energy to new roles
d.   disengagement from intellectual activity

3.   Which of the following statements best reflect life satisfaction for people in later adulthood? (pp. 471-472)
a.   Most older adults express a generally high level of life satisfaction.
b.   Older adults no longer expect to find new sources of life satisfaction.
c.   Because of physical and mental health problems, life satisfaction is low in later life.
d.   Life satisfaction in later life depends on one's educational background.

4.   Which of the following personality characteristics is associated with high life satisfaction in later adulthood? (pp. 473-474)
a.   optimism
b.   introversion
c.   cautiousness
d.   assertiveness

5.   In later adulthood, adaptation requires the integration of three processes: selection, optimization, and _____. (pp. 474-475)
a.   assertiveness
b.   crystallized intelligence
c.   extroversion
d.   compensation

6.   Research on changes in cognitive functioning in later life is difficult to interpret. One problem is separating effects of aging from _____. (p. 475)
a.   a concern about loss of memory
b.   age differences due to cohort factors
c.   a decline in crystallized intelligence
d.   a decline in fluid intelligence

7.   _____ memory refers to the ability to focus on a specific situation, such as a person identifying all the tasks completed the previous day. (pp. 476-477)
a.   Semantic
b.   Episodic
c.   Prospective
d.   Long-term

8.　　In contrast to formal operational thought, postformal operational thought _____. (pp. 477-478)
a.　　is best suited to scientific problem solving
b.　　is more dependent on laws of physics
c.　　integrates cognition and emotion
d.　　permits the systematic manipulation of multiple variables

9.　　The ability to bring knowledge accumulated through past learning and apply that knowledge to new situations is referred to as _____. (p. 478)
a.　　crystallized intelligence
b.　　fluid intelligence
c.　　prospective memory
d.　　sensory register

10.　　Grandpa Bill always sat in his favorite chair on the front porch. He looked forward to the grandchildren stopping by so that he could teach them to carve wood pieces and dispense his words of wisdom. According to this description, which of the following grandparent styles would Grandpa Bill be? (p. 481)
a.　　formal
b.　　funseeker
c.　　reservoir of family wisdom
d.　　distant figure

11.　　Which of the following types of intergenerational solidarity was found to be characteristic of families who tend to agree in opinions and expectations? (p. 481)
a.　　affectional solidarity
b.　　associational solidarity
c.　　consensual solidarity
d.　　structural solidarity

12.　　Which of the following has been demonstrated to be an important source of social support for children who are experiencing parental divorce? (pp. 484-485)
a.　　grandparent caregivers
b.　　pets
c.　　summer camp
d.　　younger siblings

13.　　In coping with widowhood, men often remarry while women _____. (pp. 485-486)
a.　　live with their children
b.　　become more self-sufficient
c.　　live with their deceased husband's family
d.　　become more withdrawn and socially isolated

14.　　Which of the following forms of leisure activity is most likely to be part of the lifestyle of older adults? (pp. 487-490)
a.　　computer hobbies
b.　　team sports
c.　　routine exercise or fitness program
d.　　ballroom dancing

15. Which of the following commonly stimulates thoughts about one's mortality in middle adulthood? (p. 490)
a. realizing that over half of one's life has been lived
b. experiencing divorce
c. a child's 21st birthday
d. all of these

16. Which of the following is an explanation for why older adults tend to have less anxiety about death than younger adults? Older adults _____. (pp. 490-491)
a. have less experience with death than younger adults
b. tend to be less religious and therefore have fewer sources of comfort in thinking about an afterlife
c. have spent less time reviewing their lives and therefore have more despair about past decisions
d. are more familiar with death because of the death of friends and relatives, and have done more to prepare for their own death than younger adults

17. What is one consequence associated with achieving a sense of integrity? (p. 493)
a. The ability to have an impact on others.
b. The ability to experience satisfaction from hard work.
c. The ability to face death without fear.
d. The ability to predict future events.

18. Which of the following terms refers to the process of deliberate self-reflection linked to the ability to achieve integrity? (p. 494)
a. introspection
b. crystallized intelligence
c. social support
d. identification

19. Which of the following concepts refers to a type of expert knowledge that reflects sound judgment and good advice in the face of typically high levels of uncertainty? (p. 495)
a. wisdom
b. fluid intelligence
c. reminiscence
d. disdain

20. Adjustment to retirement changes with time. Which of the following is considered the most positive period? (pp. 496-497)
a. after about a year
b. during the first six months
c. during the period from 13 to 18 months after retirement
d. two years following retirement

After completing the post-test, compare your score with your performance on the pre-test. Can you identify areas where significant new learning has taken place? If you still have questions about some sections of the chapter, read them again. Check the glossary. For additional test items, you may want to go to the Development Through Life web site found by going to http://www.psychology.wadsworth.com. If you still have questions, discuss them with your instructor.

Step Eight: Suggestions for Further Observation and Study

1. What are some unique life perspectives that emerge in later adulthood that help people achieve integrity? Read. E. Erikson, J. Erikson, and H. Kivnick's *Vital Involvement in Old Age*, NY: Norton, 1986 to help answer this question. You may also want to read an autobiography and note how introspection may have helped in the writing of the autobiography. Also, note some of the other psychosocial concepts that are illustrated in the autobiography.

2. Find out more about grandparenting. Visit The Grandparent Information Center at http://www.aarp.org/.

3. What roles do adults in the age range 60 to 75 play at your college or university? What efforts do the alumni office make to reach out to former students in this age range? What strategies are effective? Based on what you have read about later adulthood, what advice would you give to the alumni office about how to connect with the alumnae who are in later adulthood?

4. What do you think will be the special resources available to older adults in 50 years? What might be some special discoveries that will make later adulthood more psychologically satisfying? What might be some of the unique challenges to adaptation 50 years from now?

5. Find out more about types of support groups for those experiencing bereavement. Visit Group Support for Grief and Bereavement at http://www.aarp.org/griefandloss/articles/63_a.html

6. Find out more about retirement, especially for the baby boomers. Visit the report entitled, The Baby Boomers Look Ahead to Retirement at http://research.aarp.org/econ/boomer_seg_1.html

7. Learning through Technology: InfoTrac®
    For further study, explore InfoTrac® College Edition, an online library. Go to http://www.infotrac-college.com and use the pass code that came on the card with your book. To learn more, look up the following search terms and subdivisions in InfoTrac®.

LIFE SATISFACTION AND THE ELDERLY	RETIREMENT
	Psychological aspects
	Social aspects
	Statistics
INTELLIGENCE AND THE ELDERLY	Retirement Income
GRANDPARENTING	
WIDOWHOOD	
DESPAIR	
WISDOM	

CHAPTER FIFTEEN
Very Old Age (75 until Death)

Step One: Review the Chapter Outline

The Longevity Revolution
     A New Psychosocial Stage: Very Old Age
     The Gender Gap Among the Very Old
Developmental Tasks
    Coping with the Physical Changes of Aging
        Fitness
        Behavioral Slowing
        Sensory Changes
        Health, Illness, and Functional Independence
    Developing a Psychohistorical Perspective
    Traveling Unchartered Territory: Life Structures of the Very Old
        Living Arrangements
        Case Study: Mr. Z
        Gender-Role Definitions
The Psychosocial Crisis: Immortality versus Extinction
    Immortality
    Extinction
The Central Process: Social Support
    The Benefits of Social Support
    The Dynamics of Social Support
    The Social Support Network
The Prime Adaptive Ego Quality and the Core Pathology
    Confidence
    Diffidence
Applied Topic: Meeting the Needs of the Frail Elderly
    Defining Frailty
    Supporting Optimal Functioning
    The Role of the Community
    The Role of Creative Action
Chapter Summary

Step Two: Review the Chapter Objectives

- To identify very old age as a unique developmental period for those of unusual longevity, a stage with its own developmental tasks and psychosocial crisis.
- To describe some of the physical changes associated with aging, including changes in fitness, behavioral slowing, sensory changes, and vulnerability to illness, and the challenges these changes pose for continued psychosocial well-being.
- To develop the concept of an altered perspective on time and history that emerges among the long-lived.

- To explore elements of the lifestyle structure for the very old, especially living arrangements and gender role behaviors.
- To identify and describe the psychosocial crisis of immortality versus extinction, the central process of social support, the prime adaptive ego quality of confidence, and the core pathology of diffidence.
- To apply research and theory to concerns about meeting the needs of the frail elderly.

Step Three: Take the Pre-Test

Answer these true/false questions before you read the chapter. The pages where material is discussed are indicated after each question. Use your performance as a guide to areas where you need to read especially carefully. The Answer Key for the pre-test can be found at the end of the study guide.

_____1.   In 2050, the life expectancy at birth is projected to be 85 in the United States. (p. 504)

_____2.   The period of very old age was identified in Erikson's original conceptualization of the eight stages of life. (p. 505)

_____3.   Individual differences increase among older populations. (p. 506)

_____4.   A majority of adults who are over age 75 have many physical limitations and rely heavily on others for carrying out tasks of daily life. (p. 507)

_____5.   According to statistics regarding the gender gap in the very old, there are more men than women who are over age 75. (pp. 506-507)

_____6.   Age-related, behavioral slowing is more readily observable on routine tasks than on complex tasks that require mental processing. (pp. 508-509)

_____7.   As one ages, visual adaptation becomes easier because the pupil size increases allowing more light to reach the retina. (pp. 510-511)

_____8.   Vision and hearing are the only sense modalities that are vulnerable to age-related changes. (pp. 510-512)

_____9.   With age, greater intensity of stimulation is required to make the same impact on the sensory system that was once achieved with lower levels of stimulation. (p. 511)

_____10.   One of the age-related changes for human adults is that the number of taste buds in one's mouth decreases as one gets older. (p. 511)

_____11.   As a result of an improved immune system with age, older adults have an increased capacity to fight off infections. (pp. 512-513)

_____12. The need for assistance in daily living tasks peaks around age 70 and then declines as one increases in age. (pp. 513-514)

_____13. A person with Alzheimer's disease experiences sudden and dramatic loss of cognitive functioning over a matter of a few days. (pp. 512-514)

_____14. In acute brain syndromes, the onset of confusion is relatively sudden. Often this pattern is associated with a severe illness such as heart failure, alcoholism, or extreme malnutrition. (pp. 512-514)

_____15. A psychohistorical perspective involves the creative integration of the salient events of one's past history with the demands of current reality. (p. 514)

_____16. All individuals are part of the psychosocial evolution process in which succeeding generations receive information from previous generations. (pp. 514-515)

_____17. People who are successful agers are careful not to challenge themselves too much or to participate in activities that require complex problem solving. (p. 516)

_____18. More widowed women are likely to live alone than are widowed men. (p. 518)

_____19. Most older adults live in their home communities rather than moving to a new state. (p. 519)

_____20. Older adults who have a spouse and children are less likely to be placed in a nursing home than older adults who live alone. (pp. 520-521)

_____21. The fastest growing component of the Medicare program is community based long-term health care. (pp. 519-521)

_____22. At every age, men tend to value instrumental activities that have an achievement focus more than women do. (p. 522)

_____23. Elderly who view the end of life as bringing new forms of connection and continuity are categorized as achieving a sense of extinction. (p. 525)

_____24. Erikson's advice on coping with aging emphasizes "letting go" in order to remain optimally flexible. (pp. 525-527)

_____25. In the U.S., people in very old age have larger social support networks than do younger adults. (pp. 527-528)

Step Four: Read Chapter 15: Very Old Age (age 75 until death)

Step Five: Review the Basic Concepts By Matching Each Term and Its Definition

a. immortality   b. extinction
c. confidence   d. diffidence
e. behavioral slowing   f. psychohistorical perspective
g. social support   h. optimal functioning
i. collective efficacy   j. gender role convergence

1. _____   The level of performance of which one is capable at the highest level of motivation and preparation.

2. _____   A transformation in which men and women become more androgynous and more similar in gender orientation during later life.

3. _____   Transcendence of death through a sense of symbolic continuity.

4. _____   Age-related delay in speed and response to stimuli.

5. _____   A strong sense of social cohesion with a high level of informal social control in a community.

6. _____   The inability to act as a result of overwhelming self-doubt.

7. _____   Information leading people to believe that they are valued and part of a larger network of mutual obligation.

8. _____   A conscious trust in oneself and in the meaningfulness of life.

9. _____   An integration of past, present, and future time with respect to personal and societal continuity and change.

10. _____   A sense that the end of life is the end of all continuity and connection to the future.

Step Six: Answer the Focusing Questions

1. What is the longevity revolution? What are the implications of this revolution for the psychosocial stage of very old age? (pp. 504-505)

2.   What are the three developmental tasks associated with very old age? How do they contribute to the resolution of the psychosocial crisis of immortality versus extinction? (pp. 507-525)

3.   What are the challenges that behavioral slowing, sensory change, and vulnerability to illness and chronic conditions pose to individuals in very old age? What are some examples of coping strategies that promote high levels of functional independence in the face of these challenges? (pp. 508-512)

4.   What is a psychohistorical perspective? How does a psychohistorical perspective contribute to a sense of immortality? (pp. 514-516)

5.   Describe the living arrangements of older adults and the implications of decisions about where to live for optimizing functioning in later life. (pp. 517-521)

6.   Evaluate the concept of gender-role convergence in later adulthood. How do gender-role attitudes and behaviors appear to change in very old age? How are they consistent with attitudes and behaviors of earlier stages of adulthood? (pp. 522-525)

7.   What are the five ways to achieve a sense of immortality? (pp. 525-526)

8.   What are five ideas for promoting optimal functioning among the frail elderly? (pp. 532-534)

Step Seven: Take the Post-Test

1.   What is meant by the term *longevity revolution*? (pp. 504-505)
   a.   Older adults are staging protests, demanding more support for Medicare and social security benefits.
   b.   Older adults are refusing to pay taxes because too much of their money is going to the support of prisons and not enough to health care.
   c.   Life expectancy increased by 50% in the 20th century, resulting in a large percentage of people who live far beyond their reproductive and childrearing age.
   d.   Through medical research the life span has been extended from 120 to 150 years.

2.   Which of the following is NOT a developmental task associated with very old age? (p. 507)
   a.   coping with physical changes of aging
   b.   dealing with an organic brain disorder, such as Alzheimer's Disease
   c.   developing a psychohistorical perspective
   d.   creating new life structures

3.   Many age-related symptoms such as fatigue, weakness, and lack of resilience are related to _____.
      (pp. 507-508)
      a.   malnutrition
      b.   genetic diseases
      c.   developmental consequences of aging
      d.   declining sensory capacities

4.   Which of the following statements about changes in fitness associated with the aging process is
      most accurate? (p. 507)
      a.   70-year-olds are stronger and have greater physical endurance than 30-year-olds
      b.   With age, the need for calories increases.
      c.   The circulatory system becomes more efficient at supplying oxygenated blood to the body
            with age.
      d.   The strength and capacity for moderate effort in physical activities is about the same at age
            70 as it was at age 40.

5.   Age-related behavioral slowing is _____. (pp. 508-509)
      a.   more readily noticeable in routine tasks of daily living
      b.   associated with educational background
      c.   related to taste-smell age-related changes
      d.   more readily noticeable in complex task

6.   According to the U.S. Government's report, *Healthy People 2010,* what is the most important
      thing older adults can do to promote their physical well-being? (pp. 507-508).
      a.   eat less salt
      b.   get at least 30 minutes of physical activity daily
      c.   get at least 8 hours of sleep every night
      d.   drink more water

7.   One of the most common markers of aging that is observed in motor responses, reaction time, and
      information processing is _____. (pp. 508-510)
      a.   clumsiness
      b.   increased autonomy
      c.   behavioral slowing
      d.   rapid adaptation

8.   Which of the following sensory changes occurs after age 70? (p. 510)
      a.   sharp loss in pitch discrimination
      b.   inability to distinguish red from green
      c.   improved distance perception
      d.   improved ability to detect bitter tastes

9.   Which of the following terms refers to the ability to integrate past, present, and future and to relate
      these concepts to patterns of continuity and change within a culture? (p. 514)
      a.   optimal ability
      b.   immortality
      c.   psychohistorical perspective
      d.   role reversal

10. Studies confirm that _____ helps support an older adult's sense of well-being. (pp. 516-517)
    a. participating in intellectually complex and challenging activities
    b. letting others take over one's daily responsibilities
    c. living alone
    d. watching television

11. Which of the following statements best characterizes the living arrangements of women aged 75 and over? (p. 518).
    a. The majority live in their own home with their adult children.
    b. The majority live alone in their own home.
    c. The majority live in their own home with their spouse.
    d. The majority live in an assisted living arrangement.

12. Which term refers to a residential setting offering housing, medical and preventive health care, and social services to residents who are well at the time they enter? (p. 520)
    a. hospice
    b. continuing-care community
    c. gentrification
    d. nursing home

13. Which of the following best describes the concept of *gender-role convergence*? (pp. 522-523)
    a. Gender roles become more rigid and traditional with age.
    b. Gender roles become more idealized with age.
    c. Gender roles become more androgynous for men and women with age.
    d. Gender roles for men and women become more competitive with age.

14. Research indicates that when widows and widowers have good social support networks _____. (p. 524)
    a. they are both less interested in remarriage
    b. widows are more likely to remarry than widowers
    c. widowers tend to marry someone from their social support network
    d. widows date people from their social support network

15. A positive resolution of the psychosocial crisis of very old age occurs when people symbolically transcend death through a sense of confidence in the continuity of life. This reflects a psychosocial sense of _____. (pp. 525-526)
    a. intimacy
    b. social support
    c. optimal functioning
    d. immortality

16. What brings about the psychosocial crisis of immortality versus extinction? (p. 525)
    a. developing a point of view about death
    b. outliving one's cohort
    c. having grandchildren
    d. retirement

17. Social support contributes to well-being in three ways which include reducing isolation, providing resources, and _____. (p. 528)
    a.   building endurance
    b.   creating gender-role flexibility
    c.   traveling unchartered territory
    d.   reducing the impact of stressors

18. One of the challenges in managing the social support network is to minimize the effects of _____. (p. 529)
    a.   negative social interactions
    b.   harmonious interactions
    c.   reciprocity
    d.   function optimazation

19. What is *optimal functioning*? (p. 532)
    a.   one's achievements at age 20
    b.   the individual with the best performance within a group
    c.   the level of performance a person is able to achieve when he/she is highly motivated and prepared
    d.   the usual level of performance a person is able to achieve without special preparation or encouragement

20. What should be the primary goal of providing services to the elderly? (pp. 532-533)
    a.   to get older adults to live more like 50 year olds
    b.   to encourage older adults to give up their independence
    c.   to relieve older adults of decision-making responsibilities.
    d.   to support optimal functioning

After completing the post-test, compare your score with your performance on the pre-test. Can you identify areas where significant new learning has taken place? If you still have questions about some sections of the chapter, read them again. Check the glossary. For additional test items, you may want to go to the *Development Through Life* web site found at http://www.psychology.wadsworth.com. If you still have questions, discuss them with your instructor.

Step Eight: Suggestions for Further Observation and Study

1. Falls are a leading cause of injury among older adults. Examine your parents' current residence as a living arrangement for someone in his or her 80's. What are the risks of falling in this setting? In what ways would this setting support optimal functioning? What might be some problems your parent(s) might face if they continue living in this setting when they reach very old age? How might the setting be modified to help sustain independence in very old age?

2. Interview someone who is 75 years old or older. Ask them to tell you about the ways that their life has changed over the past twenty years. What have been the greatest challenges of very old age? How have they coped with these challenges? What are some of their greatest sources of daily life satisfaction?

3.   Visit a continuing care community and/or a nursing home. What is the daily routine for people who live in this setting? What are their relationships like with people on the staff? What aspects of the setting are designed to foster and maintain optimal functioning for the very old? What aspects of the setting interfere with optimal functioning? How may a resident maintain his/her social support network in this setting?

4.   Go to the web page of the Administration on Aging entitled Elders and Families at http://www.aoa.dhhs.gov/eldfam/eldfam.asp. Take time to explore two or three areas to learn about programs, career opportunities, and resources for aging adults and their families.

5.   Learning Through Technology: InfoTrac®
      For further study explore InfoTrac® College Edition, an online library. Go to http://infotrac-college.com and use the pass code that came on the card with your book. Look up the following search terms and subdivisions in InfoTrac® to learn more about these topics:

LONGEVITY   FITNESS AND THE ELDERY
      Analysis   Healthy Elderly
      Economic Analysis
                                       DEPENDENCY AND THE ELDERLY
FORCASTS
      Psychological Aspects   HOUSING AND THE ELDERLY
                                             Multigenerational Households
IMMORTALITY   Aging in Place

SOCIAL NETWORKS AND THE   THE FRAIL ELDERLY
ELDERLY   Collective Efficacy

CHAPTER SIXTEEN
Understanding Death, Dying, and Bereavement

Step One: Review the Chapter Outline

Mortality and Psychosocial Development
Definitions of Death
The Process of Dying
      Case Study: Too Late to Die Young
    The Good Death
    Hospice Care
    Euthanasia
    Ethical Issues at the End of Life
Death-Related Rituals
    Care of the Body
    Care of the Spirit
    Care of the Surviving Family, Friends, and Community
Grief and Bereavement
    Definitions
    Grief Work
    Five Patterns of Bereavement Among Widows
    Factors that Effect the Stress of Survivors
        Unacknowledged and Stigmatized Loss
Psychosocial Growth Through Bereavement
Chapter Summary

Step Two: Review the Chapter Objectives

- To understand the role of mortality in shaping psychosocial development
- To define the biological state of death
- To describe factors associated with the process of dying and the modern ideal of a good death
- To describe death-related rituals and their functions
- To analyze factors that affect grief and bereavement

Step Three: Take the Pre-Test

Answer these true/false questions before you read the chapter. The pages where material is discussed are indicated in the parentheses after each question. Use your performance as a guide to areas where you need to read especially carefully. The Answer Key for the pre-test can be found at the end of the study guide.

_____1.   Mortology is the field of science that studies issues of death and dying. (p. 538)

_____2.   A person's beliefs about death influence ego development at various stages of psychosocial development. (pp. 538-539)

_____3.   Developing a point of view about death is a developmental task of middle adulthood. (p. 539)

_____4.   Cardiopulmonary death is defined by two criteria: lack of a heartbeat and lack of respiration. (p. 539)

_____5.   It is impossible for a person's brainstem functions to continue when there is no cortical functioning. (p. 539)

_____6.   It is legal to remove an organ for transplant from a person who has been in a persistent vegetative state for a year. (p. 540)

_____7.   The dying trajectory refers to the time during which the person's health goes from good to death. (p. 540)

_____8.   Death always involves a high degree of suffering. (p. 541)

_____9.   The death of a child may be seen as tragic in the mind of caregivers while the death of an older person may be seen as the natural close to a full life. (p. 541)

_____10.   According to the Hospice Education Institute, one of the goals of high quality end-of-life care is offering a support system to help patients live as actively as possible until death. (p. 543)

_____11.   The majority of Americans die at home. (p. 541)

_____12.   Research has shown that people who are dying are concerned about planning their funeral. (pp. 540-542)

_____13.   Physician assisted suicide is illegal in all fifty states in the United States. (p. 544)

_____14.   In Islamic families, the burial of a dead relative takes place a full week after the person's death. (p. 546)

_____15.   Hindus believe that at death a person's spirit leaves the body and enters a small flame that is lit next to the body. On the tenth day after cremation of the body, the flame with the spirit is placed in the sea as a signal to the spirit to leave the attachments of the earthly life and begin the transition to the afterlife. (p. 546)

_____16.   A society's death rituals are important for helping the people who remain cope with their grief and reorient their lives in a world without the person who died. (pp. 546-547)

_____17.   In a study of family members who were responsible for caring for a person who died, one aspect of grief that was reported involved sensory illusions that led to the impression that the deceased person was still present. (pp. 546-548)

_____18.   According to Erich Lindemann's analysis of grief, the strategy of avoiding grief is the best one survivors can use to get through the grieving process quickly. (p. 549)

_____19.   The depression and confusion that accompany grieving may make the survivor more vulnerable to physical and mental health problems. (pp. 549-550)

_____20. Research confirms that, among older adults, one may expect a full resolution of the grief work associated with the death of a spouse in approximately 36 months. (pp. 549-550)

_____21. In a study of bereavement among widows, chronic grievers were people whose spouses had died a long, slow death. (p. 550)

_____22. Bereavement may be difficult if the survivor has experienced many positive benefits of caregiving. (p.550)

_____23. Ambiguous deaths are those in which people attribute death to an immoral, illegal, or evil cause. (p. 551)

_____24. Death by suicide is an example of a stigmatized death. (p. 552)

_____25. The death of someone whose presence serves to help you define your identity will require a redefinition of your identity. (p. 553)

Step Four: Read Chapter 16: Understanding Death, Dying, and Bereavement

Step Five: Review Basic Concepts By Matching Each Term and Its Definition

a. thanatology
b. cardiopulmonary death
c. persistent vegetative state
d. living will
e. hospice
f. passive euthanasia
g. physician assisted suicide
h. bereavement
i. grief work
j. ambiguous loss

1. _____ A condition of death in which death is uncertain because there is no verification of death as when a soldier is missing in action or there is no body, or when a person is physically present but unable to participate in any meaningful way in interactions with others.

2. _____ The long-term process of adjustment to the death of a loved one that is more all-encompassing than grief and commonly accompanied by physical symptoms, role loss, and a variety of intense emotions, including anger, sorrow, anxiety, and depression.

3. _____ The criteria for death in which there is lack of a heartbeat and lack of respiration.

4. _____ A person's psychological efforts to cope with the reality of loss of a loved one.

5. _____ An integrated system of medicine, nursing, counseling, and spiritual care for the terminally ill and his/her family.

6. _____ A document instructing physicians, relatives, or others to refrain from the use of extraordinary measures, such as life support equipment, to prolong one's life in the event of a terminal illness.

7. _____ Withholding treatment or removing life-sustaining nourishment and breathing aids for the dying person with the result that death occurs more quickly than if these procedures were continued.

8. _____ A person's brainstem functions to continue to maintain heartbeat and respiration even when there is no cortical functioning.

9. _____ The administration of a lethal dose of some medication by a physician or arranging for a terminally ill patient to administer his or her own lethal dose of medication.

10. _____ The field of science that addresses dying and death, as well as the psychological mechanisms of coping with them.

Step Six: Answer the Focusing Question

1. Give examples of how death might give meaning to life at four different stages of development. (pp. 538-539)

2. Explain the difference between cardiopulmonary death and whole brain death. (pp. 539-540)

3. Discuss three factors that help us understand some of the differences people experience in the process of dying. (p. 540)

4.   Explain what is meant by a "good death". How does hospice help achieve a good death? (pp. 542-543)

5.   Give four examples of cultural approaches to death-related rituals. What are the functions of these rituals? (pp. 545-548)

6.   What does research tell us about factors that influence the process of adjusting to the death of a loved one? (pp. 549-551)

Step Seven: Take the Post-Test

1.   Who wrote a book that suggested that people learn to talk about their fears of dying and plan for their funerals in order to face death more openly and directly? (p. 539)
       a.   Erik Erikson
       b.   Elizabeth Kübler-Ross
       c.   Robert Binstock
       d.   Anna Freud

2.   Which of the following is NOT considered a criteria for the determination of whole-brain death? (pp. 539-540)
       a.   lack of responsiveness except to the most painful stimuli
       b.   no eye movements, blinking, or pupil responses
       c.   a flat electroencephalogram (EEG) for at least ten minutes
       d.   no postural activity, swallowing, yawning, or vocalizing

3.   What is the condition called in which a person's brainstem functions continue even when there is no cortical functioning? (p. 540)
        a.   cardiopulmonary death
        b.   partial brain death
        c.   cerebral miscarriage
        d.   persistent vegetative state

4.   What is the document called in which a person can direct a physician or a hospital to withhold life-sustaining procedures and prevent the use of unwanted medical procedures when the person is unable to convey his/her wishes? (p. 540)
        a.   an attorney directive
        b.   a uniform determination of death
        c.   a living will
        d.   a deposition

5.   The time during which the person's health goes from good to death is called _____. (p. 540)
        a.   the dying trajectory
        b.   the omega period
        c.   the death convoy
        d.   the thanatos stage

6.   The primary causes of death are different for people of different ages. What is a primary cause of death for adolescents? (p. 541)
        a.   AIDS
        b.   automobile accidents
        c.   diabetes
        d.   lung cancer

7.   In some cultures the death of a child is seen as especially painful because it results in the loss of _____. (p. 542)
        a.   potential for the future
        b.   earning capability
        c.   wisdom for the society
        d.   guidance for younger generations

8.   Which of the following is NOT considered to be a goal of high quality end-of-life care? (p. 542)
        a.   promoting relief from pain
        b.   integrating the psychological and spiritual aspects of patient care
        c.   offering a support system to help patients live as actively as possible until death
        d.   helping the family plan appropriate religious services

9.   According to Carr's research about spouses reactions to their partners' death, which of the following was associated with the greatest stress for the survivor? (p. 542)
        a.   being with the partner at the moment of death
        b.   seeing the partner in great pain at the end of life
        c.   believing their partner was aware he/she was going to die
        d.   taking care of the partner's clothing and other possessions

10. _____ is an integrated system of medicine, nursing, counseling, and spiritual care for the dying person and his or her family. Its goal is to achieve the highest possible quality of life for the dying person and the family. (p. 543)
   a. Hospital
   b. Pain Clinic
   c. Hospice
   d. Ambulatory Care Unit

11. Which of the following terms refers to withholding treatment or removing life-sustaining nourishment from a patient with the result that death occurs more quickly than if these procedures were continued? (pp. 543-544)
   a. active euthanasia
   b. passive euthanasia
   c. negligent malpractice
   d. expedient termination

12. The death-related rituals of a culture usually address three critical aspects of death. Which of the following is NOT one of these? (p. 545)
   a. disposal of the dead person's possessions
   b. appropriate care of the body
   c. care of the dead person's soul or spirit
   d. how to meet the emotional needs of the survivors and the community as a whole

13. Which of the following is most accurate concerning death-related rituals? (p. 545)
   a. Burial takes place as soon as possible after death.
   b. Most societies embalm their dead.
   c. Most cultures have funerals for the dead.
   d. There is a seven day mourning period after the funeral.

14. In Amish communities, _____. (p. 548)
   a. dying people are cared for in a hospital or hospice
   b. the funeral service emphasizes that the death marks the end of existence
   c. families do not speak about the dying process or its impact on the family
   d. there is continuing support for the bereaved for at least a year following the funeral

15. Which of the following is one of the three phases of the grieving process described by psychiatrist Erich Lindemann? (p. 549)
   a. making an adjustment to all the aspects of the environment from which the deceased is missing
   b. avoiding the emotions and physical distress that accompany the death
   c. experiencing a period of physical illness
   d. being a pallbearer at the funeral

16. In a study comparing older widows and widowers with adults who were not experiencing bereavement, one of the findings was that _____. (p. 550)
   a. grieving spouses could expect to finish grieving within a year
   b. there was no difference between the two groups on alcohol use
   c. older adults learn to accept a certain empty place in their hearts for their deceased partner and find appropriate times to experience a profound sense of loss
   d. non-widowed older adults had happier marriages

17. When a person is missing and may be dead, but there are no physical remains, the family experiences _____. (p. 551)
    a.   ambivalent loss
    b.   ambiguous loss
    c.   stigmatized loss
    d.   meaningless loss

18. Following a death, there are some people who grieve but who may not be recognized as legitimate mourners. They are referred to as _____. (pp. 551-552)
    a.   unacknowledged mourners
    b.   ambiguous mourners
    c.   façade mourners
    d.   stigmatized mourners

19. Which of the following is an example of a stigmatized death? (pp. 552-553)
    a.   a murder victim
    b.   suicide
    c.   whole brain death
    d.   death following a prayer of forgiveness

20. Which of the following is an example of a way bereavement may stimulate psychosocial growth? (pp. 553-554)
    a.   It may help one understand a deeper level of emotion.
    b.   It may lead to a growth in a person's commitment to those who are in their radius of significant relationships.
    c.   It may cause a person to redefine their identity.
    d.   All of these.

After completing the post-test, compare your score with your performance on the pre-test. Can you identify areas where significant new learning has taken place? If you still have questions about some sections of the chapter, read them again. Check the glossary. For additional test items, go to the *Development Through Life* web site found at http://www.psychology.wadsworth.com. If you still have questions, discuss them with your instructor.

Step Eight: Suggestions for Further Observation and Study

1. Write a description of what you would like to have happen at your funeral.

2. Read 10 obituaries and analyze the information in these texts. What are some of the common themes that tend to be included in these narratives?

3. Interview a family member to learn about the death-related rituals that are practiced in their cultural group. Seek out additional readings about these practices in order to learn more about their origins and functions.

4. Visit the website www.uslivingwillregitry.com where you can read more about advance directives and fill out an advance directive for the state where you reside if you wish.

5. Learning through Technology: InfoTrac®

For further study, explore InfoTrac® College Edition, an online library. Go to http://www.infotrac-college.com and use the pass code that came on the card with your book. To learn more, look up the following search terms and subdivisions in InfoTrac®.

BRAIN DEATH

PERSISTENT VEGETATIVE STATE

GRIEF

BEREAVEMENT

DEATH RITUALS
    Funerals

AMBIGUOUS DEATH

HOSPICE

ADVANCE DIRECTIVES
    Living Will
    Durable Power of Attorney

Answer Key to Study Guide

Chapter One: The Development Through Life Perspective

<table>
<tr><td colspan="4">Pre-Test</td><td>Matching</td><td colspan="4">Post-Test</td></tr>
<tr><td>1.</td><td>true</td><td>14.</td><td>false</td><td>1.   e</td><td>1.</td><td>b</td><td>11.</td><td>b</td></tr>
<tr><td>2.</td><td>false</td><td>15.</td><td>false</td><td>2.   g</td><td>2.</td><td>d</td><td>12.</td><td>c</td></tr>
<tr><td>3.</td><td>false</td><td>16.</td><td>false</td><td>3.   b</td><td>3.</td><td>c</td><td>13.</td><td>a</td></tr>
<tr><td>4.</td><td>true</td><td>17.</td><td>false</td><td>4.   d</td><td>4.</td><td>a</td><td>14.</td><td>d</td></tr>
<tr><td>5.</td><td>true</td><td>18.</td><td>false</td><td>5.   f</td><td>5.</td><td>a</td><td>15.</td><td>b</td></tr>
<tr><td>6.</td><td>false</td><td>19.</td><td>true</td><td>6.   a</td><td>6.</td><td>b</td><td>16.</td><td>d</td></tr>
<tr><td>7.</td><td>true</td><td>20.</td><td>true</td><td></td><td>7.</td><td>a</td><td>17.</td><td>a</td></tr>
<tr><td>8.</td><td>false</td><td>21.</td><td>true</td><td></td><td>8.</td><td>c</td><td>18.</td><td>d</td></tr>
<tr><td>9.</td><td>true</td><td>22.</td><td>true</td><td></td><td>9.</td><td>d</td><td>19.</td><td>c</td></tr>
<tr><td>10.</td><td>false</td><td>23.</td><td>true</td><td></td><td>10.</td><td>d</td><td>20.</td><td>a</td></tr>
<tr><td>11.</td><td>false</td><td>24.</td><td>false</td><td></td><td></td><td></td><td></td><td></td></tr>
<tr><td>12.</td><td>true</td><td>25.</td><td>false</td><td></td><td></td><td></td><td></td><td></td></tr>
<tr><td>13.</td><td>true</td><td></td><td></td><td></td><td></td><td></td><td></td><td></td></tr>
</table>

Chapter Two: The Research Process

<table>
<tr><td colspan="4">Pre-Test</td><td>Matching</td><td colspan="4">Post-Test</td></tr>
<tr><td>1.</td><td>false</td><td>14.</td><td>false</td><td>1.   h</td><td>1.</td><td>c</td><td>11.</td><td>d</td></tr>
<tr><td>2.</td><td>true</td><td>15.</td><td>true</td><td>2.   j</td><td>2.</td><td>d</td><td>12.</td><td>a</td></tr>
<tr><td>3.</td><td>false</td><td>16.</td><td>false</td><td>3.   d</td><td>3.</td><td>a</td><td>13.</td><td>b</td></tr>
<tr><td>4.</td><td>false</td><td>17.</td><td>true</td><td>4.   a</td><td>4.</td><td>b</td><td>14.</td><td>d</td></tr>
<tr><td>5.</td><td>true</td><td>18.</td><td>true</td><td>5.   k</td><td>5.</td><td>c</td><td>15.</td><td>a</td></tr>
<tr><td>6.</td><td>false</td><td>19.</td><td>false</td><td>6.   b</td><td>6.</td><td>d</td><td>16.</td><td>c</td></tr>
<tr><td>7.</td><td>true</td><td>20.</td><td>true</td><td>7.   l</td><td>7.</td><td>c</td><td>17.</td><td>b</td></tr>
<tr><td>8.</td><td>false</td><td>21.</td><td>false</td><td>8.   g</td><td>8.</td><td>b</td><td>18.</td><td>b</td></tr>
<tr><td>9.</td><td>true</td><td>22.</td><td>true</td><td>9.   c</td><td>9.</td><td>c</td><td>19.</td><td>c</td></tr>
<tr><td>10.</td><td>true</td><td>23.</td><td>true</td><td>10.   e</td><td>10.</td><td>a</td><td>20.</td><td>a</td></tr>
<tr><td>11.</td><td>true</td><td>24.</td><td>true</td><td>11.   i</td><td></td><td></td><td></td><td></td></tr>
<tr><td>12.</td><td>false</td><td>25.</td><td>false</td><td>12.   f</td><td></td><td></td><td></td><td></td></tr>
<tr><td>13.</td><td>false</td><td></td><td></td><td></td><td></td><td></td><td></td><td></td></tr>
</table>

Chapter Three: Psychosocial Theory

<table>
<tr><td colspan="4">Pre-Test</td><td>Matching</td><td colspan="4">Post-Test</td></tr>
<tr><td>1.</td><td>false</td><td>14.</td><td>false</td><td>1.   b</td><td>1.</td><td>d</td><td>11.</td><td>d</td></tr>
<tr><td>2.</td><td>true</td><td>15.</td><td>true</td><td>2.   g</td><td>2.</td><td>c</td><td>12.</td><td>b</td></tr>
<tr><td>3.</td><td>true</td><td>16.</td><td>true</td><td>3.   j</td><td>3.</td><td>a</td><td>13.</td><td>a</td></tr>
<tr><td>4.</td><td>false</td><td>17.</td><td>true</td><td>4.   e</td><td>4.</td><td>c</td><td>14.</td><td>c</td></tr>
<tr><td>5.</td><td>true</td><td>18.</td><td>false</td><td>5.   d</td><td>5.</td><td>b</td><td>15.</td><td>a</td></tr>
<tr><td>6.</td><td>true</td><td>19.</td><td>false</td><td>6.   i</td><td>6.</td><td>a</td><td>16.</td><td>c</td></tr>
<tr><td>7.</td><td>false</td><td>20.</td><td>true</td><td>7.   f</td><td>7.</td><td>d</td><td>17.</td><td>c</td></tr>
<tr><td>8.</td><td>true</td><td>21.</td><td>false</td><td>8.   c</td><td>8.</td><td>b</td><td>18.</td><td>a</td></tr>
<tr><td>9.</td><td>true</td><td>22.</td><td>true</td><td>9.   h</td><td>9.</td><td>c</td><td>19.</td><td>b</td></tr>
<tr><td>10.</td><td>false</td><td>23.</td><td>false</td><td>10.   a</td><td>10.</td><td>c</td><td>20.</td><td>d</td></tr>
<tr><td>11.</td><td>false</td><td>24.</td><td>true</td><td></td><td></td><td></td><td></td><td></td></tr>
<tr><td>12.</td><td>true</td><td>25.</td><td>false</td><td></td><td></td><td></td><td></td><td></td></tr>
<tr><td>13.</td><td>true</td><td></td><td></td><td></td><td></td><td></td><td></td><td></td></tr>
</table>

Chapter Four: Major Theories for Understanding Human Development

Pre-Test				Matching		Post-Test			
1.	true	14.	false	1.	l	1.	b	11.	c
2.	true	15.	true	2.	m	2.	b	12.	b
3.	true	16.	true	3.	b	3.	a	13.	c
4.	false	17.	false	4.	c	4.	c	14.	d
5.	false	18.	false	5.	g	5.	d	15.	a
6.	false	19.	true	6.	a	6.	a	16.	c
7.	true	20.	false	7.	e	7.	b	17.	c
8.	false	21.	false	8.	f	8.	d	18.	a
9.	true	22.	true	9.	n	9.	b	19.	d
10.	true	23.	false	10.	h	10.	c	20.	c
11.	false	24.	true	11.	j				
12.	false	25.	false	12.	d				
13.	true			13.	k				
				14.	i				

Chapter Five: The Period of Pregnancy and Prenatal Development

Pre-Test				Matching		Post-Test			
1.	true	14.	true	1.	g	1.	a	11.	d
2.	false	15.	false	2.	c	2.	b	12.	d
3.	true	16.	false	3.	j	3.	b	13.	d
4.	false	17.	true	4.	a	4.	d	14.	c
5.	true	18.	false	5.	h	5.	d	15.	d
6.	true	19.	false	6.	e	6.	b	16.	c
7.	true	20.	true	7.	d	7.	c	17.	d
8.	false	21.	false	8.	i	8.	c	18.	b
9.	true	22.	true	9.	l	9.	c	19.	d
10.	true	23.	false	10.	f	10.	a	20.	b
11.	false	24.	false	11.	b				
12.	true	25.	false	12.	k				
13.	false								

Chapter Six: Infancy (First 24 months)

Pre-Test				Matching		Post-Test			
1.	false	14.	false	1.	k	1.	a	11.	a
2.	false	15.	true	2.	h	2.	b	12.	a
3.	true	16.	false	3.	a	3.	b	13.	a
4.	true	17.	true	4.	g	4.	b	14.	a
5.	false	18.	true	5.	c	5.	b	15.	c
6.	true	19.	false	6.	f	6.	c	16.	d
7.	true	20.	true	7.	j	7.	b	17.	c
8.	false	21.	true	8.	i	8.	c	18.	c
9.	true	22.	true	9.	l	9.	b	19.	d
10.	false	23.	false	10.	b	10.	b	20.	b
11.	false	24.	false	11.	d				
12.	true	25.	true	12.	e				
13.	false								

Chapter Seven: Toddlerhood (Ages 2 and 3)

Pre-Test		Matching	Post-Test	
1. true	14. false	1. b	1. a	11. a
2. true	15. false	2. e	2. d	12. c
3. true	16. false	3. h	3. a	13. c
4. false	17. false	4. i	4. d	14. b
5. true	18. true	5. a	5. c	15. b
6. false	19. false	6. c	6. a	16. c
7. false	20. false	7. l	7. a	17. d
8. true	21. false	8. d	8. b	18. c
9. false	22. false	9. k	9. c	19. c
10. true	23. true	10. g	10. c	20. d
11. true	24. true	11. j		
12. false	25. false	12. f		
13. true				

Chapter Eight: Early School Age (4 to 6 years)

Pre-Test		Matching	Post-Test	
1. true	14. false	1. j	1. c	11. d
2. false	15. false	2. b	2. a	12. d
3. true	16. true	3. e	3. a	13. c
4. false	17. false	4. a	4. c	14. c
5. true	18. true	5. c	5. c	15. c
6. false	19. true	6. i	6. a	16. b
7. false	20. true	7. f	7. a	17. b
8. false	21. false	8. g	8. b	18. b
9. true	22. false	9. h	9. d	19. a
10. true	23. false	10. d	10. a	20. a
11. false	24. true	11. l		
12. true	25. true	12. k		
13. false				

Chapter Nine: Middle Childhood (6-12 Years)

Pre-Test		Matching	Post-Test	
1. true	14. true	1. d	1. c	11. a
2. false	15. true	2. c	2. c	12. a
3. true	16. true	3. a	3. b	13. d
4. false	17. false	4. f	4. b	14. b
5. true	18. false	5. b	5. b	15. d
6. false	19. false	6. i	6. c	16. d
7. true	20. false	7. e	7. a	17. b
8. true	21. true	8. k	8. a	18. b
9. false	22. false	9. g	9. c	19. b
10. false	23. false	10. j	10. b	20. b
11. false	24. true	11. h		
12. true	25. true			
13. false				

Chapter Ten: Early Adolescence (12 to 18 years)

Pre-Test		Matching	Post-Test	
1. true	14. false	1. h	1. b	11. d
2. false	15. false	2. a	2. a	12. b
3. false	16. false	3. i	3. a	13. c
4. true	17. true	4. g	4. d	14. a
5. true	18. true	5. e	5. c	15. b
6. false	19. true	6. b	6. c	16. b
7. true	20. true	7. l	7. d	17. d
8. true	21. false	8. c	8. d	18. c
9. false	22. false	9. k	9. d	19. a
10. true	23. true	10. f	10. a	20. b
11. false	24. true	11. j		
12. true	25. true	12. d		
13. false				

Chapter Eleven: Later Adolescence (18 to 24 years)

Pre-Test		Matching	Post-Test	
1. false	14. true	1. c	1. c	11. b
2. true	15. false	2. g	2. c	12. b
3. true	16. true	3. h	3. a	13. c
4. false	17. true	4. b	4. a	14. b
5. true	18. true	5. d	5. d	15. d
6. false	19. false	6. j	6. d	16. d
7. false	20. false	7. k	7. a	17. b
8. true	21. true	8. a	8. b	18. d
9. true	22. false	9. e	9. d	19. c
10. true	23. false	10. f	10. a	20. d
11. true	24. false	11. l		
12. true	25. false	12. i		
13. false				

Chapter Twelve: Early Adulthood (24-34 Years)

Pre-Test		Matching	Post-Test	
1. true	14. false	1. k	1. b	11. c
2. true	15. true	2. c	2. b	12. a
3. false	16. false	3. d	3. d	13. c
4. true	17. false	4. e	4. b	14. a
5. true	18. false	5. g	5. d	15. d
6. true	19. false	6. f	6. b	16. c
7. false	20. true	7. i	7. a	17. d
8. false	21. true	8. b	8. a	18. a
9. false	22. true	9. l	9. c	19. c
10. true	23. false	10. h	10. d	20. a
11. true	24. false	11. a		
12. true	25. false	12. j		
13. false				

Chapter Thirteen: Middle Adulthood (34-60 years)

Pre-Test				Matching		Post-Test			
1.	false	14.	false	1.	d	1.	a	11.	b
2.	true	15.	false	2.	h	2.	b	12.	c
3.	false	16.	true	3.	e	3.	d	13.	d
4.	true	17.	false	4.	i	4.	d	14.	a
5.	false	18.	true	5.	g	5.	b	15.	b
6.	true	19.	false	6.	c	6.	a	16.	d
7.	false	20.	false	7.	l	7.	c	17.	c
8.	true	21.	true	8.	b	8.	b	18.	d
9.	false	22.	true	9.	j	9.	d	19.	c
10.	true	23.	false	10.	a	10.	a	20.	a
11.	true	24.	true	11.	k				
12.	false	25.	false	12.	f				
13.	false								

Chapter Fourteen: Later Adulthood (60-75 years)

Pre-Test				Matching		Post-Test			
1.	true	14.	true	1.	k	1.	a	11.	c
2.	false	15.	true	2.	d	2.	d	12.	a
3.	true	16.	true	3.	g	3.	a	13.	b
4.	true	17.	false	4.	i	4.	a	14.	c
5.	true	18.	false	5.	f	5.	d	15.	a
6.	false	19.	true	6.	e	6.	b	16.	d
7.	false	20.	true	7.	a	7.	b	17.	c
8.	false	21.	false	8.	h	8.	c	18.	a
9.	true	22.	true	9.	l	9.	a	19.	a
10.	true	23.	true	10.	b	10.	c	20.	b
11.	true	24.	false	11.	c				
12.	false	25.	false	12.	j				
13.	false								

Chapter Fifteen: Very Old Age (75 until death)

Pre-Test				Matching		Post-Test			
1.	true	14.	true	1.	h	1.	c	11.	b
2.	false	15.	true	2.	j	2.	b	12.	b
3.	true	16.	true	3.	a	3.	a	13.	c
4.	false	17.	false	4.	e	4.	d	14.	a
5.	false	18.	true	5.	i	5.	d	15.	d
6.	false	19.	true	6.	d	6.	b	16.	b
7.	false	20.	true	7.	g	7.	c	17.	d
8.	false	21.	true	8.	c	8.	a	18.	a
9.	true	22.	true	9.	f	9.	c	19.	c
10.	true	23.	false	10.	b	10.	a	20.	d
11.	false	24.	true						
12.	false	25.	false						
13.	false								

Chapter Sixteen: Understanding Death, Dying, and Bereavement

1.	false	14.	false						
2.	true	15.	true						
3.	false	16.	true						
4.	true	17.	true						
5.	false	18.	false						
6.	false	19.	true						
7.	true	20.	false						
8.	false	21.	false						
9.	true	22.	true						
10.	true	23.	false						
11.	false	24.	true						
12.	true	25.	true						
13.	false								

Pre-Test

1.	false
2.	true
3.	false
4.	true
5.	false
6.	false
7.	true
8.	false
9.	true
10.	true
11.	false
12.	true
13.	false
14.	false
15.	true
16.	true
17.	true
18.	false
19.	true
20.	false
21.	false
22.	true
23.	false
24.	true
25.	true

Matching

1.	j
2.	h
3.	b
4.	i
5.	e
6.	d
7.	f
8.	c
9.	g
10.	a

Post-Test

1.	b	11.	b
2.	a	12.	a
3.	d	13.	c
4.	c	14.	d
5.	a	15.	a
6.	b	16.	c
7.	a	17.	b
8.	d	18.	a
9.	b	19.	b
10.	c	20.	d